charge
up your life

Other books in the Charge Up Your Life series

Charge Up Your Life Workbook: Over 100 Tools to Explore and Discover the Real You

Charge Up Your Life Journal: Guided Daily Writings

Charge Up Your Life for Teens and Young Adults (upcoming)

Charge Up Your Life for Parents (upcoming)

charge
up your life

Conquer the 6 barriers to love,
happiness, and success

Ellen M. Diana, PhD
Connie M. Leach, EdD

Illustrated by Stacy Lynn Coleman

Charge Up Your Life: Conquer the 6 Barriers to Love, Happiness, and Success

Published by Wheatmark®
610 East Delano Street, Suite 104
Tucson, Arizona 85705 U.S.A.
www.wheatmark.com

ISBN: 978-1-60494-509-6 (paperback)
ISBN: 978-1-60494-586-7 (Kindle)
LCCN: 2010933812

Dedication

We dedicate this book to Everett, Hayden, and Peyton, our beautiful grandchildren. They enrich our lives, energize us, and give us hope for a bright future.

Table of Contents

C

Compliment and Nurture
5

H

Here and Now
39

A

Accept Your Possibilities
75

R

Respectful Relationships
113

G

Genuine and Authentic
151

E

Enjoy and Experience Life
187

Reading Group Guide
237

Disclaimer

The information and exercises in this book are not intended to be a substitute for therapy. They are designed to be tools for self-exploration.

Introduction

Dear Reader,

What holds you back from living the life you want? Identifying the barriers that keep you stuck and obtaining the tools to break through these barriers are the keys to bringing love, happiness, and success into your life. The Charge Up Your Life method is the essential tool to start you on your way because it defines the six critical barriers that ultimately hinder success and offers simple, step-by-step solutions for each barrier. This book provides information on each barrier and self-awareness exercise to help you experience each solution in a very personal way.

The word "Charge" in the title represents the energy and action needed to move you closer to your goals. Motivation and inspiration will help you to become the best you can be! Charge is also an acronym, with each letter corresponding to a catchy phrase that will help you remember how to overcome each of the six barriers. These six solutions will help you to conquer the obstacles that keep you stuck and feeling discouraged. On the following page is a condensed and easy-to-follow outline of the Charge Up Your Life model:

The Phrase and Focus	The Barrier	The Solution
C Compliment and Nurture	Self-Criticism	Self-Nurturance
H Here and Now	Anxiety and Stress	Focused Awareness
A Accept your Possibilities	Self-Limiting Beliefs	Unlimited Possibilities
R Respectful Relationships	Conflict	Harmony
G Genuine and Authentic	Unhealthy Boundaries	Integrity
E Enjoy and Experience Life	Despair	Hope

Before you begin to read the chapters, take the quiz on page 1 to identify your personal barriers. As you read each chapter, work through the exercises, and gather tools for success; your self-awareness will be altered and you will notice your life in ways you hadn't previously. Before you begin to read, you might jot down several areas of your life that you feel need work and that you are interested in "changing." At the end of each chapter are pages where you can chart your progress, plan your future goals, and access resources for further support. After you complete the book, you'll see how you have acquired the tools you need to actualize your hopes and dreams.

Why This Book Was Written

The Charge Up Your Life personal growth system grew from Ellen and Connie's personal experiences. Both had lost their fathers early in life and were raised by single mothers, who struggled to raise a family during a time when there was little social support for widows or fatherless children. Ellen and Connie grew up feeling they were inferior to and different from other children, which led to low self-confidence, anxiety and stress, and depressive thinking.

Because of their common experiences, they joined efforts to share with others their personal journey of healing and self-discovery which developed into the Charge Up Your Life model.

The authors of *Charge Up Your Life* bring a wealth of professional experience to its writing. Ellen has worked as a psychologist, both in private practice as well as in public and private schools, for over twenty-five years. Connie is a life coach with degrees in educational administration and counseling, and over twenty-five years of experience as an elementary and middle school teacher and administrator. Through their work, both found that most often individuals, families, and couples are seeking love, happiness, and success. Some of their situations were more serious than others, but the underlying barriers were the same for all people. By working through these six underlying barriers (low self-esteem, inability to manage anxiety, self-limiting behavior, ineffective social skills, poor interpersonal boundaries, and negative thinking), individuals could easily reach their personal goals as well as enrich and energize their lives.

Ellen and Connie applied two major theoretical concepts, from their training in Gestalt therapy, in creating the Charge Up Your Life method: First, the Paradoxical Theory of Change states that "change occurs when one becomes what he is, not when he tries to become what he is not" (Arnold Beisser). So, putting yourself on a plan of improvement is not likely to be successful; however, by improving self-awareness and working to be the best you can be, positive change naturally follows. Second, Gestalt therapy theory teaches through doing, not only by talking, because to understand something and incorporate it into your life, you need to experience it, not just talk about it. Thus, the activities in the book take you, the reader, step by step through the solution to each of the six barriers in a very personal yet interactive manner.

We hope that you enjoy this journey of self-discovery as much as we have enjoyed developing these tools for you.

Enjoy!
Ellen and Connie

Charge Up Your Life
Self-Check Quiz

Take this brief quiz to identify what holds you back. Directions: Put a check in front of the items that are true for you. Respond as quickly as possible without over thinking your responses.

_____ 1. I have more weaknesses than strengths.

_____ 2. I worry about the future.

_____ 3. I should change some things about myself.

_____ 4. I feel taken advantage of at home and work.

_____ 5. Sometimes I'm afraid to be honest with others.

_____ 6. I often feel helpless and hopeless about situations in my life.

_____ 7. I don't feel positive about my future.

_____ 8. I find it hard to be around others who don't share my beliefs.

_____ 9. Not many people know the real me.

_____ 10. I feel that people I'm close to should know what I need without my having to tell them.

_____ 11. I often criticize myself.

_____ 12. Sometimes I overreact to situations.

_____ 13. I am not often curious about or interested in others' ideas and opinions.

_____ 14. I can't stop thinking about past mistakes or failures.

_____ 15. I feel sad a lot of the time.

_____ 16. I often ask for advice before making a decision.

_____ 17. I tend to avoid dealing with my problems.

_____ 18. I don't accept compliments or help from others very well.

_____ 19. I feel like I'm good at giving advice.

_____ 20. I am a perfectionist.

_____ 21. I see most people as being very different from me.

_____ 22. I often overlook my body's signals of stress, anxiety, fatigue, anger, and sadness.

_____ 23. I feel alone and disconnected from others.

_____ 24. I don't always say what I really mean.

_____ 25. I often use the words "should" or "have to."

_____ 26. I don't like the way I look.

_____ 27. I find it hard to relax.

_____ 28. I often skip meals or eat whatever is quick and available.

_____ 29. I worry about pleasing others more than I worry about pleasing myself.

_____ 30. There are some people I just don't like.

Scoring the Quiz:

Circle the numbers below that correspond to the statements you checked:

C - 11, 16, 18, 26, 28; H - 2, 12, 14, 22, 27; A - 1, 3, 20, 25, 30; R - 8, 10, 13, 19, 21; G - 4, 5, 9, 24, 29; E - 6, 7, 15, 17, 23.

Count the number of items in each of the six letter categories and notice the ones that have 2 or more circled. These are the areas that keep you stuck.

C	Low Self-Confidence
H	Anxiety and Stress
A	Self-Limiting Beliefs
R	Conflicted Relationships
G	Unhealthy Boundaries
E	Depression and Negative Thinking

Now notice the categories that have zero or one circled. These areas may be ones in which you have fewer challenges. As you read through each chapter, you'll acquire the tools to conquer your personal barriers to love, happiness, and success.

$\mathscr{C}$

Compliment and Nurture

Self-Criticism ◄——► Self-Nurturance

- Know Your Worth
- Increase Your Self-Knowledge
- Strengthen Your Self-Support
- Appreciate Yourself

"Give yourself what you need."

"I'm good enough,
I'm smart enough,
and doggone it,
people like me."

—*Al Franken as Stuart Smalley on Saturday Night Live*

C: Compliment and Nurture

Self-Criticism ◄———► Self-Nurturance

Introduction

Myra was a thirty-year-old interior designer. She was well educated and experienced in her field; she had talent and poise, as well as excellent interpersonal skills, but she lacked self-confidence. On the job, she deferred to everyone else because she was afraid to make a mistake and didn't want to look bad in front of her colleagues and customers. To her bosses, Myra often seemed timid and unsure, even though they encouraged her to take risks and rely on her own instincts. Myra didn't feel she was "good enough" or as good as others on her design team. She focused on what she lacked rather than on the talents she possessed. When coworkers complimented her on a well-designed project, Myra would point out the deficiencies and deflect the praise directed at her. Myra suffered from low self-esteem and didn't see her strengths as others did.

Poor self-esteem often creates debilitating and self-defeating circumstances. Self-esteem is built on self-worth which is not dependent on accomplishments, but instead is based on an intrinsic sense of personal value. When you feel valued for who you are, rather than for what you achieve, your self-esteem and confidence will grow.

Like Myra, do you often criticize yourself either out loud or silently? Does a negative inner voice tell you that you're not doing things correctly or you're not **measuring up?** Perhaps you have trouble treating yourself to nice things or leaving a job that you don't like. Maybe you have difficulty accepting compliments and praise or lack confidence in your own judgment, so you rely on others to make decisions for you. If you see yourself in any of these situations, then low self-esteem could be a barrier for you, as shown below in the story of Sam.

> Sam played soccer on a city league with some long-time friends. He was a competent player because he had some natural athletic ability; however, he wasn't a great player. He never scored the winning goal and he wasn't the go-to guy for passing the ball, so he consistently devalued his contribution to the team. He believed his friends asked him to join the team simply because it would have been awkward to exclude him. He failed to see that his friends genuinely liked him and saw him as a great guy, a fun person with whom they enjoyed spending time. His worth as their friend and his value as a teammate didn't depend on his soccer skills. Sam's low self-esteem prevented him from seeing this. He believed he needed to be a star in order to be valued.

Self-esteem isn't composed solely of the areas in which you excel and the skills that you've acquired. It encompasses everything about you. This includes your likes and dislikes, traits and skills, as well as all other aspects that make you unique. When you know who you are, you are then able to support yourself by appreciating your preferences and satisfying your needs. This is often difficult because you don't want to appear self-involved or self-centered, however, providing self-support is not about being selfish. Self-support is about taking good care of yourself and communicates a sense of self-love and the belief that you deserve the bounty of good things life has to offer. Thus, the ability to be able to receive from life, feeling deserving, and being compassionate toward oneself, are necessary components of healthy self-esteem and confidence.

Self-criticism, that negative inner voice that tells you that you aren't measuring up, can create physical, emotional, and spiritual trauma. It can undermine the most talented individuals' attempts to find love, happiness, and success. However, healthy self-esteem and confidence can propel the most average of individuals down a confident and determined path to living a happy life. Self-esteem is the foundation of everything you build your life on and, for that reason, it is the first issue addressed in this book.

Self-Worth, Self-Knowledge, Self-Support, and Self-Appreciation are the four elements that make up healthy self-esteem. In this chapter, C—Compliment and Nurture, you will learn to conquer self-criticism, this first and most important barrier to obtaining love, happiness, and success in your life.

In this chapter, you will learn to recognize that you are unique and irreplaceable. You'll get to know more about yourself and practice having the things in life that make you happy. You'll learn that the hallmark of high self-esteem is being open to receiving "gifts" from others. When you complete this section you'll understand how to Charge Up Your Life by nurturing your unique self.

C
The Nurturing Parent Experience

Imagine what it would be like for you to have a nurturing parent with you whenever you needed support, guidance, and love. Envision a loyal, compassionate, and caring parent who would provide unconditional affection, and who would encourage you to care for yourself in healthy ways. Rather than focusing on improving your weaknesses, this nurturing parent would remind you of your strengths and help you to showcase your talents. You have the power to access this positive inner voice at any time throughout your day.

The first step in connecting with your nurturing parent is to relax and focus your thoughts inward on this positive inner voice that has always been with you. If you find it difficult, your positive inner voice may be muted by your negative inner voice, which focuses on shaming and criticizing. To diminish the power of this negativity, take a moment to consciously turn down the volume on this negative voice, which will allow your positive voice to be heard.

Next, imagine this voice as a being, perhaps someone you know such as a relative, a friend, or an actual parent, living or dead, who is consistently loving and supportive. Or your being could be someone from history, a fictional character, or someone totally of your own creation who will be uniquely yours. Now create an actual image of this being to keep with you or to display in a prominent place. For example, write a description, make a clay model, draw a picture, or find a photograph.

As you go about your day, consciously access your nurturing parent. Connect with its warmth, listen to its encouraging words, and feel its unconditional support. Practice seeking out your nurturing parent when you meet with frustration, disappointment, and conflict. Trust this loyal guide to support you in being the best that you can be.

C: Compliment and Nurture

Step One: Know Your Worth

When Cindy Crawford entered modeling she was encouraged to remove the prominent mole on her face because some felt that it detracted from her beauty and didn't conform to mainstream notions of what a super model should look like. Cindy resisted this advice and her facial mole has since become her trademark. She saw her worth just as she was.

Self-worth, the first step of C: Compliment and Nurture, is about believing that you have a right to be in the world and that you are important, unique, lovable, and irreplaceable. This is the most essential element in finding love, happiness, and success. As you work at integrating it into your personal belief system, you'll see that it is the foundation for everything you'll learn in this book.

An awareness of self-worth rests on the firm belief that you have the right to be alive and that the design of your existence is intentional, not accidental, or unplanned. Thus, you were meant to have, for example, brown hair, an aptitude for math, and a love for music. The way you were created was purposeful and deliberate and so nothing in you is missing or broken. For example, the fact that you are unable to golf well, despite lessons starting in your teens, does not indicate that you are missing some important piece. This is just the way you were made.

Because your existence is purposeful, it follows that how you came into this world is right and that you have within you all that you need to find love, happiness, and success. Your compilation of traits, qualities, and physical attributes has value just because you exist. While you might share traits, qualities, and experiences with others, your combination of them is unique. Because of this, you occupy a distinctive place in this world, one that is yours alone and that no one else can fill. You make a unique contribution that gives importance to every one of your thoughts, feelings, and actions. All of your goals and dreams have value.

Your worth as a human being is not contingent on accomplishing anything or becoming anyone of great societal importance. In our culture, we often assess an individual's value based on her net worth or occupation; e.g., millionaire, doctor, lawyer. But when we do that, what are we saying about individuals who own nothing of any value, have little or no education, have physical or mental limitations, or are employed in minimum wage occupations? Aren't we subtly judging these people as less worthy, less human? Do those individuals who do not speak, see, hear, or walk have no worth? What about those individuals who are low-functioning, chronically ill, or physically handicapped? The list is endless of how we might judge or define an individual's worth. For those who have seen the film, *The Miracle Worker*, who can forget the look of pure delight on Helen Keller's face when she understood the link between the water that was running over her fingers and the word being spelled out in her hand by her teacher, Annie Sullivan? This compassionate teacher recognized Helen Keller's value, her worth, her essence, rather than dismissing Helen because of her perceived deficiencies.

You might wonder if your self-worth could be diminished by illness or injury. If you lose an important function or ability, do you also lose your self-worth?

Christopher Reeve, the "Man of Steel" who became a quadriplegic, relied on technology for his every breath. Despite his comprehensive injuries, the essence of Christopher Reeve was undamaged and his self-worth remained intact. In his last years, he went on to champion the cause of the physically handicapped and to expand visibility for this worthy endeavor through his many influential Hollywood contacts. Thus, a change in our physical or mental circumstances during our lifetime does not diminish the essence of who we are; it does not alter our self-worth, our uniqueness.

Your worth does not need to be earned by generating a product, an expected behavior, or even a grade. Self-worth is a basic human right. When you believe your worth needs to be earned, you can feel shamed into believing that something is intrinsically wrong with you. This further weakens your sense of self. If you lack self-worth, you feel wrong at your very core and lack a firm foundation in life. Without a strong and positive sense of self-worth, your sense of self is built on shaky ground, like a skyscraper built on sand. The building might look good and function for awhile, but tumble under duress. So, too, it is with people.

Low self-worth is at the core of many abusive relationships. Abuse comes in many forms and can include neglect in the case of young children, the elderly, and the chronically ill. Abuse occurs across all ages and in all types of relationships: between friends and family members; at work with exploitive employers and coworkers; as well as with intimate partners causing the abused to feel unworthy of love and of value.

> Kathy was a thirty-seven-year-old female who was sexually and emotionally abused as a child. She was removed at age ten from her parents' care and placed in a loving foster home, where she thrived. She went on to earn a college degree, enjoy a successful career as an accountant, and have an active social life with friends. In her intimate relationships, however, she seemed to find "Mr. Wrong" over and over. Kathy chose abusive men who were controlling and self-centered, and who did not reinforce her many fine qualities. Instead, these men worked at tearing down her self-esteem with words and actions. Why would such an outwardly successful woman choose partners who did not recognize her worth and did not treat her respectfully? Deep inside Kathy never truly felt happy or content with herself, and this feeling played out in her intimate relationships. She saw herself as "damaged goods" and was blocked from seeing her core self-worth because of the depth of her shame over not feeling good or right or complete.

While low self-worth is often connected to abusive relationships, not all individuals who have low self-worth are victims of abuse. However, people everywhere can benefit from looking closely at their self-worth by noticing how they allow others to treat them. When you endure subtle indignities, such as unkind words, condescending actions, or disrespect, deep down there is a part of you that feels undeserving of better treatment.

> In the movie Legally Blonde, Elle Woods is a young woman in a relationship with a young man who does not see her worth. He demeans her in-

telligence and her potential as a human being. She follows him to law school and initially buys into the stereotype of what a Harvard law student should be like, which makes her feel ashamed and inadequate. She doesn't fit the mold, and her self-esteem suffers. It is only when she gets in touch with her self-worth and supports her true essence that she is able to reach her potential and find a mate who appreciates her true spirit.

When you appreciate the richness of the human race and see worth in yourself, and in every individual you encounter, you increase the depth of your own personality and add to the richness of your own existence. The result is that your thoughts become measured and deliberate; you don't rush to judge or compare. Your actions, by default, become loving and compassionate. You find less to mock in another person who is different from yourself because you know differences communicate richness and not flaws. You also extend that degree of respect to yourself, and you begin to see your value and will nurture and love yourself.

When you recognize that you are worthwhile and practice respect in your daily life, you take the first step in developing healthy self-esteem and realizing your hopes and dreams. When you believe that you are worthwhile and that you have a right to be alive just as you are, then you will attract love, happiness, respect, and success because you'll believe that you deserve it.

Charge Up Exercise One
Know Your Worth!

Increase your self-worth by doing the following activities:

1. As you go about your day, notice your own distinctive qualities. What makes you rare and irreplaceable? What gifts do you possess? What makes you lovable? What traits and qualities can you take in and love about yourself? Recognize how each one of your thoughts, feelings, and actions contributes to the world in a unique manner. Notice your worth.

_____

_____

_____

2. Review all the contacts you made today with friends, family, coworkers, grocery clerks, neighbors, and any other people with whom you interacted. Notice your contribution, even something as simple as a smile offered to a passer-by on the street. How would the world have been different if you had not been alive? Notice your worth.

_____

_____

_____

C: Compliment and Nurture

Step Two: Increase Your Self-Knowledge

Debbie lacked self-confidence and typically deferred to her self-assured husband on most decisions. When ordering in a restaurant she would often ask her husband, "Would I like that?" rather than considering her own preferences. She simply did not know her own mind. When she shopped for clothes, she always went with her poised and polished sister who made the final decisions on all purchases. **Debbie spoke to her mother everyday and discussed any issue she had with family or friends. Her mother was only too pleased** *to offer advice to her timid daughter, just as she always had. Debbie had, in fact, more than a few strong-willed, confident people in her life. She saw them as being better at knowing her than she was.*

The next step in developing self-esteem and confidence is to make a concerted effort to get to know yourself better. Often you can live your life day to day mindlessly without truly being aware of what you are doing. Routines take over and you live unconsciously. But now is the time to increase your self-acceptance and esteem by becoming aware of your identity, your inner qualities, strengths, talents, preferences, values, desires, and feelings.

Everything you think, feel, and do has worth and says something important about you. Each reaction, opinion, or emotion is interpreted by your personal filter, and no one else in the world perceives things quite the way you do. People who are close to you may assume they understand you or can interpret your actions, because they feel they know you well; however, it's important to recognize that you are the only expert on you. So, getting to know yourself, through conscious awareness of your thoughts, feelings, and actions, is a very personal activity that only you can do on your journey to healthy self-esteem.

Vicki was unexcited about life. She had difficulty describing herself and didn't see that she was special or unique in any way. Vicki grew up in a home where pleasing her parents was her number one job. They expected Vicki to agree with their opinions and share their interests. As a result, Vicki never got to know much about herself because she got little validation and support for being an individual. As an adult, this left Vicki lacking confidence with a dire need for self-knowledge.

Getting to know your preferences is important because each of your likes and dislikes communicates information about your identity, both your intrinsic nature **and the person you show to the world.** Nurturing yourself involves recognizing your personal preferences and embracing them, so spend time noticing what you like and dislike. Become aware of how you are living your life and the effect that each of your choices has on it. When you express a preference for something, whether it's a job, a movie, or a political candidate, you are honoring your being, and showing appreciation for your individuality.

Often, you might not know your preferences, because you haven't thought consciously about them, or you defer to others to determine them for you rather than taking ownership of your own choices.

Charge Up Your Life by getting to know what you love and what you don't! What colors do you enjoy having around you and what colors do you dislike? What types of clothes do you like wearing? What fabrics feel good on your body and which ones don't? Discover your identity, your essence, your unique stamp on the world. Be curious about the many decisions that you make about yourself every day. What new things can you notice about yourself?

Your identity is your essence, your uniqueness in the world. It's comprised of many elements that, in combination, define you as a unique individual. Pay attention to who you are and how you came to be. First, notice your physical appearance. Are you tall, short, heavyset, or slender? What color are your eyes and hair?

When June first decided to try coloring her gray hair herself, she was stumped at deciding what color to purchase. She couldn't decide if she should buy dark blonde, light brown, ash, or golden hues because she had simply never noticed her hair that closely. She had gone forty years without taking in what color her hair was. So take the time to notice yourself and appreciate what you see.

Consider other identifiers such as food preferences that are often shaped by ethnicity and tradition. It is likely that as you left your family and merged with others in marriage or cohabitation you blended these preferences with your partner's and friends', or, if you lived alone, you developed your own personal style. You carried on some traditions while you phased out others. Notice preferences around food. What foods do you enjoy? Which ones do you dislike? Do you ever find yourself eating food you really dislike out of habit or because others around you are eating it? In what ways are your food preferences a factor of your upbringing or that of your mate's? Consider whether your choices of food are conscious ones.

> Chun is an Asian-American woman with olive skin and dark hair and eyes. She is of medium height and build and always maintained her weight easily with a healthy Asian diet and regular exercise. However, when Chun married her Italian husband, who loved pasta dishes with rich sauces, Chun changed her eating as it was just easier to cook one meal than to prepare two separate meals. Chun noticed a significant weight gain and realized that this selection of foods was not working well for her metabolically.

Also, consider your leisure time pursuits, which also might have been shaped by family interests and activities you were exposed to in your youth. For example, Janice's family loves basketball and they get together to watch the "March Madness" collegiate playoffs annually. They can be identified by this shared interest. They look forward to this activity and it bonds them as a family unit. The camaraderie of the event, as well as the basketball itself, generates good feelings for family togetherness. Other families might enjoy camping and boating, and still others prefer reading and listening to music. What traditions did your family have that you continue to honor and which ones did you abandon? Notice how you developed into the person you are today.

The activities that you were exposed to at home might have helped you to determine your career interests. Was it a mindful or an unconscious decision? Did you choose your occupation to please someone else or because you **truly loved it?**

> Greg's father, sister, uncle, grandfather and several cousins were all accountants in the family business. They each had skill in mathematics that they applied to this occupation. Greg pursued accounting not only because of a shared family skill, but also because of the exposure that the profession received within his family. He received detailed information on the ins and outs of the job as he listened to family members discuss their work. He noticed that the profession created feelings of satisfaction in his relatives, and Greg got inside information on how to succeed in it.

Another way you identify yourself is by the roles that you play.

> Yesenia defines herself as the sister of Juan and the daughter of Esperanza and Miguel, and as a mechanical engineer. She is also a member of the local businesswomen's association. Yesenia is only one of many mechanical engineers in her company as well as one of many professional women in her business organization, so these identifiers define Yesenia in very general ways to others but they are uniquely combined in her.

How would you define yourself by the roles you play? Notice the ways you are visible to the world. Do they communicate your essence?

Your traits and qualities, as well as your skills and abilities, define you. Some are acquired by genetics, others by environmental influences. The questions to ask in order to get to know yourself better are endless. The exercise that follows offers a sample of questions and examples that may help you better understand and define your identity which will, in turn, move you toward a strong sense of self-acceptance. Notice yourself. Take time to get to know you.

Charge Up Exercise Two
Increase Your Self-Knowledge!

Charge Up Your Life by truly knowing yourself. Start by creating a journal. You may want to purchase a portfolio, notebook, or create something of your own. Title this journal, "My Bank Account of Virtues," and make the following deposits:

1. List at least 50 of your positive qualities and personal preferences. As you go about your day, notice your likes and dislikes, your preferences, and opinions. Anything you notice about yourself is important because it expresses your uniqueness in the world. For example, you may have let someone in front of you in line at the grocery store, so add "generous" or "courteous" to your list. Perhaps you admired an outfit someone was wearing, and so you could add "like bright colors" to your list. Every detail you notice about yourself is important.

2. Add to your list the leisure activities and hobbies you enjoy; the foods and flavors you prefer; and the colors, smells, textures, and sounds you love. Stretch and challenge yourself by delving deep into your preferences and joys.

3. Now think of the environments you find most comfortable and enjoyable? This could be a place in nature, a particular building, or a place in your home. In what places do you find comfort and solace? In what places do you feel happy?

If you have difficulty generating a list of virtues, try finishing the following sentences:

I am aware that I like . . .

I enjoy . . .

I have a good time when . . .

It feels good when I . . .

I enjoy going to . . .

I like being with . . .

My favorite foods are . . .

When I need to relax I like to . . .

The trait I like best about myself is . . .

The type of movies I enjoy are . . .

I feel energized when I . . .

I enjoy talking to people who . . .

I express my creativity by . . .

Three things I need every day are . . .

Friends most often say that I am . . .

I try to avoid . . .

C: Compliment and Nurture

Step Three: Strengthen Your Self-Support

Jade wanted to be a psychologist for as long as she could remember. She pored over the "Dear Abby" column each day and avidly read the magazine Psychology Today from the age of fourteen, long before she was able to decipher many of the terms used. When it came time for college and she announced that she'd like to be a psychology major her mother remarked sarcastically, "What do you think you're going to do with that degree?" Jade felt shamed. During her first psychology class she found many things to criticize and devalue about the subject. She ended up switching her major to education, one which met with her mother's approval. However, when it came time to earn her master's as a mature adult, she saw that her goal to be a psychologist was a worthy one that expressed her unique essence.

Once you recognize your self-worth and acquire self-knowledge, it is important to use that information to give yourself those things you desire and need — physically, mentally, emotionally, and spiritually. You may worry that others will perceive you as narcissitic or selfish if you provide self-support, however, giving yourself what you need isn't about taking away from others. Self-support is simply about taking good care of yourself. How to take care of your needs in relationship with others is addressed in chapter "G: Genuine and Authentic" under the topic of interpersonal boundaries. For right now, stay focused on you and what you need to feel happy, successful, and loved. It is your number one job in this life to be the best you can be, by loving yourself, and living the happiest and most successful life you can.

To start, ask yourself whether you allow yourself to have the things that make you happy. For example, do you buy yourself that special item you've always wanted? Do you provide yourself with the time you need to exercise or care for your health? In other words, how good are you at giving to yourself? When you're good at supporting yourself, you know what you like and are able to express your choices and get your needs met.

As an extreme example of self-support, think of a baby who sees himself as the only person in the whole world. His every action is focused on obtaining what he needs to feel satisfied in the moment. Babies know what feels good and what doesn't and are vocal, although unsophisticated, in communicating those needs. When the need is unmet the baby cries and when the need is met the baby smiles. This shows that babies are in contact with their needs.

As you grow, you are taught to delay, repress, and sometimes even deny your needs. This can be both positive and negative. On the positive side, it is a sign of maturity to balance and prioritize multiple needs. You know that you need to work in order to pay your bills and have money for a vacation. Thus, you balance your need for leisure with your need for security. On the negative side, you can become so used to disregarding your needs that you become numb and detached from the knowledge of what you need to feel loved, happy, and successful.

When you become aware of what you need to thrive and freely support yourself, your self-esteem grows. When you do not allow yourself to have what you need, your self-esteem erodes. **Physical complaints, fatigue, depression, anxiety, and general unhappiness can result when you do not show love for yourself by providing regular doses of self-support and nurturance.**

The list of ways you can nurture yourself is long, varies from person to person, and contains both big and small things. The list of big things may include focusing on your physical well-being by giving yourself the proper diet, sufficient sleep, and regular exercise you need. Attending to your mental, emotional, and spiritual well-being might include spending time with people who value you, engaging in hobbies or sports that interest you, and having a career that is challenging and rewarding. Nurturing also involves small, daily things like taking a ten-minute break at work when you need it, pushing the snooze button on your alarm for an extra fifteen minutes of much-needed sleep, taking a long bubble bath, sticking up for yourself when you are being criticized, wearing your favorite shirt to work just because it makes you feel good, or letting your family know you just aren't in the mood for a pasta dinner tonight.

You nurture yourself and provide self-support when you attend to your needs in the moment in a loving way. Bodily needs are the easiest to understand; when you are hungry or thirsty, it is nurturing to eat or drink. Mental, emotional, or spiritual needs are just as important, and are also expressed through the body; however, you need to listen carefully to your body to recognize these needs. Do you ever feel mentally weary, emotionally drained, or spiritually depleted? How does your body communicate these feelings to you? Perhaps you can't concentrate, feel irritable, catch a cold, or get a sinus infection. Do you simply plod on or do you stop to attend to that need, perhaps by seeking out a friend to talk to, listening to an inspirational speaker, consulting with a physician, or meditating? How do you find solace? Listen to your body. It's asking for support. Provide it by nurturing yourself and you'll see the physical symptoms of eroding self-esteem decrease or disappear altogether.

Behavioral excesses involving drugs, alcohol, eating, gambling, spending, sex, work, and even exercise can be attempts to bolster low self-esteem. When you do not provide self-support, you may try to escape the situation through a behavioral excess. Think of the stressed-out eater, the individual who needs a drug or a few drinks to reduce social anxiety, the compulsive shopper who needs something new to feel good after a setback, the overachiever, or the workaholic. They overcompensate for their lack of good feelings about themselves. How do you bolster your self-esteem when it is ebbing? What do you turn to when you are feeling insecure or inadequate? Notice when you are drawn to one of these behaviors. What unmet needs are you trying to satisfy, or from what strong feelings are you trying to escape? When you are able to display your needs in a healthy way and provide support to get them met, then you reduce the need to indulge in behavioral excesses.

Finally, if you don't know how to give to yourself by supporting your basic needs, you may not be physically or emotionally able to give to others. Your personal needs must be met before you can attend to the needs of another person. For example, on airlines, the flight attendants instruct adult passengers to apply their own oxygen masks first, before assisting children or other adults. Much in the same way, understanding, nurturing, and providing for yourself is necessary before you are able to give to others in a healthy way.

In addition, when you deny your needs, you may find that you actually give others what you truly would like to have for yourself. For example, have you ever found yourself giving a gift to someone that you would like to have received yourself? Perhaps you've purchased sweets or treats for your family only to find that you were the only one eating them. What did you need or want at these times? It can be difficult to perceive someone else's needs if you are blinded by your own need for self-support. Give to yourself in loving, nurturing ways, both large and small every day, and watch your self-esteem flourish.

Charge Up Exercise Three
Strengthen Your Self-Support!

Support your needs by trying out several of the following:

1. Make time to be with others who share your interests and who appreciate and support you just as you are. Take time to be with people you enjoy and whose company energizes you.

2. Do things you enjoy: watch a favorite TV program, meet a friend for lunch, meditate, work on a special project, read an interesting book, take a walk, work out, or prepare a special meal. Immerse yourself in the things you love.

3. Focus on your physical well-being through proper diet, sufficient sleep, and regular exercise. If you're unsure of what to do, consult with a healthcare professional or a personal trainer.

4. Find an eating plan that works with your body type and personal preferences and makes you feel comfortable in your own skin. A nutritionist can help find a plan that fits you.

5. Recognize how much sleep your body needs to feel energetic and rested, and give yourself the rest you need. Avoid judging yourself for what you are not doing while you sleep.

6. Make a list of at least 10 activities that you enjoy and begin to incorporate them into your daily life.

C: Compliment and Nurture

Step Four: Appreciate Yourself

Johnna struggled to accept praise from others. For example, when she was complimented on her outfit, she deflected the compliment by saying, "This old thing? I've had it forever." During our weekly workshops, Johnna practiced graciously receiving compliments from her peers. She noticed the feelings that came up when she received a sincere compliment, such as "unworthy, shameful, or undeserving." She worked on taking in and internalizing the praise, warmth, and good feelings of each compliment and she rehearsed a gracious and honest response. Humility, which is a virtue, had become Johnna's Achilles heel. She began to work on balancing her generous nature with accepting the gifts and kindnesses that life offers. Her conscious awareness of her self-esteem increased.

Perhaps you've had a similar experience to Johnna's. What stopped you from taking in a sincere compliment? Did you feel deserving of the kind words? Did you worry about appearing self-centered, or did you want to appear selfless, as if you didn't need the affirmation that goes along with praise, as if you didn't need anything?

The final step in building self-esteem is to feel that you deserve to receive the abundance of good things that life has to offer. Notice how easy or hard it is for you to appreciate yourself by receiving the good things in life. Are you able to give yourself the things you truly desire, from a new pair of running shoes or the latest book by your favorite author all the way to an expensive piece of jewelry or a fancy car? Do you feel deserving? Also, can you accept things from others, even something as simple as a sincere compliment?

Achieving a balance between giving and receiving is necessary for healthy self-esteem to develop; however, many individuals starting at a young age are taught that what they want isn't important.

The importance is placed on others' needs and they are deemed "selfish" and shamed for asking for what they want. This message often yields adults with a low sense of worth who can only value themselves when they give to others. Giving to themselves triggers a shame reaction. Individuals such as these have difficulty standing up for themselves and asking for what they need and want, because they fear being viewed as selfish. Receiving from others and from the bounty that life provides is a challenge for them. Although giving to others is certainly a virtue and something most of us aspire to do, the key to healthy self-esteem is in balancing giving with receiving.

During our weekly workshops, Johnna practiced graciously receiving compliments from her peers. She noticed the feelings that came up when she received a sincere compliment, such as "unworthy, shameful, or undeserving." She worked on taking in and internalizing the praise, warmth, and good feelings of each compliment and she rehearsed a gracious and honest response. Humility, which is a virtue, had become Johnna's Achilles heel. She began to work on balancing her generous nature with accepting those gifts and kind things that life has to offer. Her conscious awareness of her self-esteem increased.

Kind and generous individuals make the world a better place for all of us. However, the urge to give must be balanced with a willingness to be open and receptive. Sometimes the balance involved in the concept of karma can also play a part for those who mostly give but don't receive. They are intent on building up points for generosity, kindness, and thoughtfulness, like a Bank Account of Virtues, but are wary of making any withdrawals, for fear that fate will turn on them. Have you ever felt that way? Have you ever gotten a bit anxious when things are going too well in your life? Do you worry about something bad happening to balance out all the good? To keep that from happening, you may have tried ways to minimize your good fortune.

> Beth likes playing all kinds of games: board games, word games, card games, computer games, and puzzles. Beth also likes gambling, and she's good at it. Her specialty is roulette, and she instinctively knows how to pick a winning number. Beth's game-playing instincts come in handy when

she hits the wheel at the local casino, and she usually wins ... but then she typically loses. At her last trip to the roulette wheel, she handily won eight hundred dollars, but rather than quit, she bet again until it was all gone. A fellow gambler, beside her at the wheel remarked ruefully to her, "I can't leave until I've lost it all, too." Beth was taken aback when she realized that this was her pattern; Beth rarely left the casino with any winnings. She had been sabotaging herself by playing until she lost all of the money she had won. She found that she rarely could leave the casino with any winnings and usually stayed until she gambled away every last dollar. Beth did not feel deserving of the winnings. Subconsciously, she believed she was undeserving of her good fortune.

Does something like this ever happen to you? When things are going your way, do you find a way to undermine yourself, sell yourself short, or pull the rug out from under yourself? If so, unconsciously, you probably don't feel deserving of having good things. What gifts or blessings do you have difficulty receiving?

If you don't feel worthy of having the good things in life, you subtly set yourself up not to have them. You might avoid applying for the great job, that you are well qualified for, and instead keep yourself in a lesser position by telling yourself that you could never get that job. That great job is for someone else. It's out of your reach. You might delay taking the last two classes you need to graduate, so that you can't get the great job that is waiting for you. There are also more subtle ways to undermine yourself, like not getting to work on time or leaving early, forgetting to get an important project in on time or delaying responding to an important client's phone call. When you repeatedly "forget," "delay," and "avoid," eventually negative things will begin to happen to you. Your partner will become annoyed or your boss angry. Your response could be indignation, anger, depression, or disappointment, but in all cases you have no one to blame but yourself. You're setting yourself up to get what you mistakenly believe you deserve.

The mark of a healthy personality is the ability to receive as well as give. When you are able to let your needs be visible to others, you open yourself up to receiving love, compliments, acknowledgment, praise, respect, money, recognition, and time. You receive these things when you believe that the universe is a bountiful place with enough good things to go around, and that it is okay for you to want, desire, and need them. Believe that you are entitled to good things in your life and allow yourself to pursue them with joy. You deserve to be loved, happy, and successful!

Charge Up Exercise Four
Appreciate Yourself!

Practice self-appreciation by doing the following:

1. Make a list of the things you have recently given to others. Which of those gifts would you like to have for yourself? Pay close attention to what you give or want to give to others — it may be what you really need. When you haven't nurtured yourself sufficiently you unconsciously project your own needs onto others. Ask yourself, "What am I giving to others that I am not receiving?" In what ways do you give to others and in what ways do you allow others to give to you? Fill out the chart below and see what you are wanting.

Gifts Given to Others	Would you have liked to receive this gift? Explain why or why not.
Ex. "Send birthday cards to friends and family."	Ex. "Enjoy receiving cards on my birthday."

2. Fill out the chart below. In the first column, list the specific ways in which you give or help others. In the second column list the specific ways in which you receive from others. Be sure to include a variety of gifts such as time, affection, praise, objects, physical contact, money, support, recognition, and so on. When you are finished, what do you notice about the two columns? Are they similar in length or is one column considerably longer than the other? Are the types of gifts similar from one column to the next, or are they unbalanced in some way? Do you find you are more comfortable giving or receiving, or are you equally comfortable doing both?

Ways I Give to Others	Ways I Let Others Give to Me
I send cards to friends on their birthdays	I let my family treat me to a massage or a day at the spa
I praise others for their hard work	I enjoy receiving compliments from coworkers
I give generously to charity	I enjoy being taken out to dinner on my birthday

Charge Up Your Life Milestones

C: Compliment and Nurture

Now that you have finished C: Compliment and Nurture, what skills have you learned and what ones are you still working on?

- Put a check mark in front of the statements that feel true to you right now.
- Put a circle in front of the statements that you have not yet achieved.

_____ I believe I am a whole and complete person who occupies a unique place in this world.

_____ I believe my worth is not contingent on generating a product.

_____ I acknowledge that I have many positive qualities and I let them shine.

_____ I take good care of myself by getting the diet, sleep, and exercise I need.

_____ I spend quality time with people who value me.

_____ I appreciate myself as I am.

_____ I nurture myself by being my own good parent and friend.

_____ I know that being good to myself does not mean I am selfish.

_____ I have hobbies and interests, and I make time to enjoy them.

_____ I believe that I deserve love, happiness, and success in my life.

_____ Every thought, feeling, and action of mine has purpose and value.

_____ I'm aware that everything I think, feel, and do passes through my personal filter.

_____ I treat myself to special things just because.

_____ I know what I need, and I take responsibility for getting it.

_____ I'm practicing "C: Compliment and Nurture" in the following ways:

_____

_____

_____

_____

_____

_____

_____

_____

_____

_____

_____

_____

_____

_____

C – Compliment and Nurture

Additional Resources

The following is a list of suggested materials to help you on your journey to healthy self-esteem:

* *The Art of Extreme Self-Care: Transform Your Life One Month at a Time* by Cheryl Richardson—12 strategies to change your life one month at a time. Learn to love, grow, and care for yourself.

* *Daring to be Yourself* by Alexandra Stoddard—Develop your personal style at home, work, and play through beauty and harmony.

* *The Power of Self-Esteem: an inspiring look at our most important psychological resource,* by Nathaniel Brandon, Ph.D. – Learn 12 obstacles to the growth of self-esteem along with his six famous self-empowerment principles.

* *Toxic Criticism: breaking the cycle with friends, family, coworkers, and yourself,* by Erin Maisel, Ph.D. – Learn to take away the power of criticism by believing in yourself.

* *Self-Esteem Companion: Simple Exercises to Help You Challenge Your Inner Critic and Celebrate Your Personal Strengths* by Matthew McKay, Ph.D.; Patrick Fanning; Carole Honey Church; Catherine Sutker – Follow a step-by-step guide to change the way you think about yourself.

"Too many people
overvalue
what they are not
and undervalue
what they are."

—*Malcolm Forbes*
Publisher, Forbes Magazine
(1919-1990)

H
Here and Now

Anxiety ◄────► Focused Awareness

- Know Where You Are
- Listen To Your Body Talk
- Keep Situations Right-Sized
- Stay Present Through Your Senses

"Stay present through your senses."

"Do not
anticipate trouble,
or worry
about what may
never happen.
Keep in the sunlight."

—Benjamin Franklin
US author, diplomat, inventor,
physicist, politician, and printer
(1706–1790)

$\mathcal{H}$: $\mathcal{H}$ere and $\mathcal{N}$ow
Anxiety ◄────► Focused Awareness

$\mathcal{I}$ntroduction

Marilyn was creative, intelligent, and highly skilled at her job in public relations. Clients enjoyed working with her because Marilyn collaborated respectfully, listened well, and intuitively knew just which marketing strategy would yield the desired results. She was great at communicating her work individually or in small groups but panic set in when she was asked to present her ideas in front of a large group. Dry mouth, accelerated heartbeat, and an inability to catch her breath made the experience unbearable. She just couldn't think. Over time, it hindered her potential for advancement and led to feelings of shame and embarrassment. Anxiety was managing Marilyn and it interfered with her ability to function effectively at work.

Anxiety is fear of the unknown and is a potent force that can keep you from realizing your full potential. It ranges from a gnawing sense of dread all the way to a full blown panic attack. Some anxiety is healthy because it keeps you safe by causing you to consider consequences before you act. **Anxiety becomes unhealthy when it interferes with your functioning in a major life activity, such as work or relationships.** Anxiety is not to be confused with the adrenaline rush an athlete might feel before a sporting event or the energy an actor might create prior to going on stage. Anxiety is debilitating and prevents you from moving forward and reaching your goals.

When you feel out of control and frozen by indecision, or **when** you constantly second guess your actions, then anxiety is managing you and coping strategies are needed. There are events that create anxiety in most people, such as the illness of a loved one, the loss of a job, or a natural disaster, but generally the list of what creates anxiety is endless and varies from person to person.

In H: Here and Now, you will learn the four steps of managing anxiety: Know Where You Are, Listen to Body Talk, Keep Situations Right-Sized, and Stay Grounded Through Your Senses. Practicing how to overcome this barrier will give you the ability to manage anxiety when it arises and to move through it successfully when it occurs. In this section you will learn that anxiety is generated by either apprehension over the future or rumination about the past. In addition, you will learn to listen to and trust the signals your body sends to alert you to feelings of anxiety. You will practice ways to stay grounded in the present moment and learn how to keep problems in their proper perspective.

H
Safe and Tranquil Experience

Take a few minutes and think of a place where you feel safe, calm and secure. Perhaps this place is somewhere you have been before or perhaps it is someplace you have never seen but would like to experience. Whatever place comes to mind, real or imagined, close your eyes and visualize yourself in this **safe and tranquil place right now. Where are you? What does your place look like? What do you see as you look all around? Notice what you smell. What sounds do you hear? What** tastes do you notice in your mouth, in the air? What do you feel with your body, your skin, arms, legs, feet, hands? Take a few more minutes to totally breathe in this experience by using all **five of** your senses.

Keeping your eyes closed, how are you feeling at this moment (relaxed, tired, energetic, hungry)? Notice your breathing. Is it shallow, deep, even, or irregular? How do your muscles and joints feel? Achy, tense, relaxed, stiff? **Notice your entire body. What is it like for you to be in this safe and tranquil place? What thoughts or memories come to mind? What, if any, emotions surface during this experience...** (happiness, sadness, pleasure, love, joy)?

Take the time to draw, sketch, or paint your **safe and tranquil place**, putting as much detail as you can into your picture. This will help further ground this experience. Notice what feelings surface as you create your tranquil place. You may want to share your creation with a friend or relative. If you do, describe the setting and the ways in which this place makes you feel safe and secure. Tell this person why you chose this special place. Think of a way to keep this image of your safe place close at hand. For example, if the beach is your safe place, you may want to carry an image of a starfish with you or post it in an important place in your home or at work. **Notice the difference in your breathing and other body sensations between when you do this exercise, and in your daily life. Your safe and tranquil place can be revisited whenever you want to feel peaceful and calm.**

H : Here and Now

Step One: Know Where You Are

During Jazzercise class, Connie's mind wanders into the past or the future as she worries about what needs to be done for the day, such as preparations for meetings or phone calls to return. She is aware of concerns over each family member's health and that she needs to find time to pay household bills and arrange for repairs. All the while, she is keeping step unconsciously to the music and following the instructor. When she notices that she is not present she gently brings herself back to the present by paying attention to her body in the here and now.

Know Where You Are is the first step in H: Here and Now. This could seem puzzling and you might ask, "Don't I always know where I am?" The answer is, "Not really." There are three time dimensions: past, present, and future, and chances are you aren't aware of how much time you spend in any one of them. This is because your mind wanders from present to past, back to the present, and then into the future, often without your conscious awareness. The present is the only time dimension where reality exists and things happen, so it's important to be aware of when you lose focus and find yourself drifting into the past or the future, ruminating over something that's already happened or anticipating something that has yet to occur. The more time you spend in the present, the less anxiety and fear you will feel. The less anxiety you feel, the more energy you will have available to work on your goals.

First, consider how often during your day you feel calm, relaxed, and peaceful. How much time do you feel in control of whatever is happening and fully committed to and focused on whatever task is in front of you? As you work at home or at your job, notice when and how often you are distracted from your task. These distractions are examples of not being in the present; your mind wandered somewhere else and you weren't attending to your present experience. Consider whether you ever started driving somewhere and suddenly found yourself at your destination, not quite knowing how you got there. Or, have you ever been reading only to find at the bottom of a page unable to recall anything that you read on that page? We've all had these mini "out of body" experiences where our minds wander, usually to something we are worrying over or concerned about. When this happens, your thoughts are no longer in the present, focusing on the activity. Your thoughts wandered to the past or the future. This is where anxiety lives.

To become more conscious of how much time you spend in the present, try this simple exercise: Find a comfortable chair and relax. Turn off whatever might be making noise around you, like the TV or radio, and just get comfortable. Pay attention to your breath. Become aware of breathing in and breathing out, nothing more. Count how many seconds you breathe in and how many seconds you breathe out. Notice if your in-hale is longer or shorter than your exhale. What's happening to you as you do this? How many seconds can you pay attention to your breath and nothing else? Where has your mind wandered off to? Have you found yourself thinking of the tasks around the house that are not done, a conversation you just had with a friend, a movie you just saw, or what's for dinner? Unless you're an experienced meditator, it's likely that you thought of something other than your breath. Once again, focus your attention on the present, notice your breath, and try not to allow your mind to wander off. The amount of time you are able to focus on your breath is the amount of time you are in the present. The rest of the time, your thoughts are either in the past or the future. It seems a simple thing to be in the present and pay attention to your breath, but it requires sustained, persistent effort.

Anxiety is generated when you ruminate over past experience or feel apprehensive about the future. Anxiety does not exist in the present moment. This may seem confusing because you may think, "I'm anxious right now!" in the present moment. But actually your mind has moved out of the present and into the past or the future. To illustrate, make a list of all the things you feel anxious, worried, or concerned about. Look at each of the items on this list and consider whether they are related to the past or the future. You might be worried about having enough money to meet your monthly expenses, whether you are doing a good job at work, or whether you'll ever find a life partner. These are future worries. You might also think: what if I hadn't taken this job, what if I had married someone else, or what if I had only finished college? These are past worries. Worries enter your mind in the present, but they pull you into thoughts of the past or the future, where anxiety lives. Even if you are involved in a dangerous situation, it is your thoughts of similar situations from your past, or your imaginings of what could happen next, that generate anxiety.

Anxiety does not necessarily occur every time your mind wanders, because not every past event is a cause for anxiety. Ruminating over an event from the past is not the same as reviewing an event from your past. When you review the past, you intentionally choose to look back to gain knowledge, consider past experiences, and connect them to your present experience. For example, you might review a route you traveled to consider whether any changes need to be made the next time you travel, or you might think back to the fun you had on a cruise you took last summer. You have chosen to bring the past into the present moment for review.

Also, purposefully planning for your future is different from having thoughts about the future that create anxiety. Planning ahead ensures that you consider obstacles you may encounter and allows you to adjust and respond to them accordingly. Anticipation, a feeling of eagerness and hope for what is to come, is another intentional look at the future. Or, you might wonder about living in the city where you've just been offered a job or daydream about how you would look driving in a new sports car. Anxiety, in contrast, is about losing control of your thoughts when you are pulled into the past or the future. Do you see the difference?

Haley, a young wife and mom, recalled feeling anxious while preparing for a holiday family dinner. She had difficulty understanding how her anxiety was related to past or future events. She argued that her anxiety existed in the present moment, "right now." She had volunteered to hold the family dinner at her new home and wanted everything to go well. She counted on having help from her mother and sister-in-law, but unforeseen events interfered. Her mom was recovering from the flu and her brother and his family were delayed in traffic. Because of these changes, Haley was imagining a disastrous outcome of her dinner party. This was something that she conjured up in her mind about future events that had not yet occurred. In order to avoid anxious thoughts, Haley needed to focus on what was actually occurring at that time by remaining present-focused. Nothing bad had happened yet, but Haley's thoughts took her into a calamitous future that caused her to feel anxious, stressed, and overwhelmed.

Another way we lose present awareness and move into thoughts of the past or future is by not allowing ourselves to be satisfied. Have you ever gotten exactly what you wanted, but then second-guessed yourself about whether you really wanted it?

Kirsten and Amos had been trying to conceive a child for over two years, consulting unsuccessfully with a well-known fertility expert. Kirsten concluded that she was tired of devoting her life to this one goal and discussed with Amos that they should focus on their careers, marriage, and travel interests and accept that they might never have children. Amos agreed with much relief. He disclosed that he believed they were over-focusing on this one aspect of their lives, but he had wanted to support her. He proposed that they just move on with their lives in other ways, much as she had proposed. But hearing this Kirsten couldn't let it go. She ruminated over whether his certainty about moving on took away her option to change her mind, her chances for adoption, or even the possibility of an unplanned pregnancy. After all, the doctor had said there was no physical reason why they couldn't conceive. So Kirsten wouldn't allow herself to be satisfied. Realistically, she and her husband were now in agreement; both had disclosed how they truly felt and found they were of one mind. This could have made her happy, but it didn't. She ruminated over whether they had tried hard enough and looked apprehensively into a future that she now imagined as empty and worthless without children.

The issues don't need to be as important and life-changing as Kirsten and Amos's. They could be smaller things like asking the boss for a raise and receiving one, and then questioning whether you should have asked for more. You might make a compromise on which movie to see but then obsess about how you really wanted to see the "other" movie, ultimately chastising yourself for not standing up for your first choice. Neither choice can be undone immediately, but your enjoyment of the moment can be diminished considerably by not being in your present experience and enjoying it. You can make a decision to ask for another raise in six months and go to see the movie you really wanted to see next weekend. These decisions allow you to enjoy the present but give you the option to plan for the future.

In a similar way, you can ignore certain changes in your life. Some adjustments are small, such as overlooking the fact that you are ten pounds heavier and need to move to the next clothing size. You can stubbornly continue to stuff yourself into clothes that are too tight and feel uncomfortable because you cannot accept that your body has changed. Some changes, however, are very serious, such as adjusting to the loss of a loved one or the loss of a job or home. You can allow your grief to overwhelm you by not dealing with the unresolved issues of your loss.

When your thoughts are unintentionally pulled into the past or future, you devote precious energy to events that are not really happening now. Energy to meet your goals is only available in the present because the present is the only place where things happen. The past is already over and can't be changed. The future has yet to come. Rumination and apprehension deplete your resources. Staying in the present allows you to focus your energy on what is actually happening and enables you to make progress toward your goals, diminishes feelings of anxiety and stress, and allows you to move toward joy and success.

Charge Up Exercise One
Know Where You Are!

Practice diminishing your anxiety by doing the following:

1. Notice when your mind pulls you into the past or into the future. As you notice your mind straying, gently redirect yourself to what is before you. Do not criticize yourself, just notice and gently focus your mind back to the present. Be aware of how often you are pulled out of the present.

2. To help raise your awareness of Knowing Where You Are, keep a log of the times your mind wandered away from the present, whether it went into the past or future, and what caused it. Describe the experience in as much detail as possible.

    Example: "Today, I noticed my mind wandering into the future when I worried about not passing the exam that I am scheduled to take next week. I imagined telling coworkers that I hadn't passed the test and felt like a loser having to say that I failed. I noticed my palms beginning to sweat and my stomach tightening into a knot. I realized I was anxious about something that had not yet occurred."

3. Notice the patterns of your worries. Perhaps you find yourself feeling apprehensive about the future or ruminating over issues from the past. Awareness is the first step in diminishing anxious feelings. Notice where your worries take you. Gently and without judgment, bring yourself back to the present. Jot down the specific worries that keep pulling you out of the present. Make an intentional effort to deal with each one of those worries and fears.

H: Here and Now

Step Two: Listen to Your Body Talk

Regina was often ill with gastrointestinal symptoms and missed work frequently until she realized that the constant knot in her stomach was her response to the ongoing interpersonal tensions in her office. Regina was a "fixer" and regularly took on others' problems. When coworkers were not getting along, she tried to intervene and mediate because she had a strong need for harmony in her environment. She worked at providing a calm home life for herself and her family with minimal discord; however, at work this was out of her control. She had choices to make about her work environment: she could stop feeling responsible for relieving the tension in the office, ask for a transfer to another department, or do some serious job hunting. Looking at this situation and noticing her needs allowed her to feel some relief and act on the initial problem proactively. Regina was learning to honor her Body Talk.

Body Talk is another way anxiety keeps you from staying focused. Body Talk is the mechanism your body uses to tell you that your equilibrium has been disturbed, and you are no longer comfortable and at ease. To listen to Body Talk you must be in the present and notice the sensations your body is experiencing. You can't hear your Body Talk when anxiety pulls you into the past or the future.

Some Body Talk is universal and easily recognizable; for example, hunger pangs cause you to eat, dry mouth signals you to drink, and a yawn or drooping eyelids invite you to rest. Body Talk tells you, through unusual muscle aches and pains, that your workout was too strenuous and communicates that you need to cut back in duration or intensity. You will generally feel better after you have recognized and satisfied your basic physical needs because your equilibrium has been re-established.

Body Talk is also individual and personal as when your body signals negative feelings. You may contract a cold when you experience ongoing stress, suffer a headache when you feel angry, or struggle with fatigue when you feel sad. Clenched hands, sweaty palms, headache, stomachache, muscle tension, tight jaw, stiff neck, butterflies in the stomach, or a feeling of light-headedness are a few of the common ways your body might communicate anxiety to you.

When you notice your personal Body Talk you can use this information to make good choices for yourself. When you don't listen to your Body Talk, unreleased tension and unresolved issues can cause actual physical ailments. Have you ever consulted with your personal physician about some physical symptoms that test after test did little to clarify? Did your physician ruefully communicate to you that she could find no true physical ailment to diagnose? Chances are, if testing was exhaustive and no diagnosis emerged, then you were experiencing Body Talk. Instead of leaving your physician's office feeling invalidated, consider what was happening in your life at the time. Was there tension in your work environment? Were you having difficulty in a relationship? Could finances have been an issue? Your body was trying to tell you something. When you experience Body Talk, discover what the underlying issues are.

Unresolved issues from the past, such as grief or trauma, can create chronic Body Talk in the present. Stuffing problems inside and not expressing your distress creates mental and emotional tension, which over time, manifests itself in physical problems. We are only beginning to recognize the link between the mind and body in chronic physical illness, such as in the case of migraine headaches. Treatment is moving away from mainstream remedies such as medications and moving into a combination of pain medication and alternative treatments such as yoga, meditation, tai chi, and acupuncture. The effectiveness of stress-reducing techniques illustrates that the body is connected to the mind, and the most successful treatment recognizes this link. If you suffer from a chronic illness, consider what tension you may be holding in as a result of over unresolved disappointments or losses from your past.

Grief in its many forms can build up inside and cause you to live in a chronic state of tension and anxiety. When this happens, even small and inconsequential events have the power to affect you physically. By allowing yourself to be present with the emotions attached to these events, you release the tension associated with them. You are able to see how your present-day life is affected by events from the past.

> Brian was a middle-aged widower and the single parent of three teenagers. He did an admirable job of juggling school and work schedules as well as volunteering at his church to provide peer counseling for members who had lost spouses, and he regularly worked out at the local gym. From time to time he surfed the web and subscribed to online dating services, but after four years, he had not found a new mate. Brian was sad because as fulfilling as parenting was, he missed having a partner. He could not understand why he was not more successful. It seemed **that every new relationship lasted for only two or three dates before each woman stopped going out with him. One day, Maria, Brian's sister, was visiting and observed him on the phone telling a potential date about his trauma caring for an invalid wife, the trials and tribulations of raising children, and the unpredictability of his work schedule and how it made it hard for anyone to accept him as he was. Maria heard the anxiety in his words and voice and saw the tension in his body as he spoke. She saw that his negativity and fear interfered with his ability to attract someone. She helped him to see that only after he dealt with his unresolved grief issues would he be able to move on to a new life.**

If you don't pay attention to your Body Talk and listen to your body's cries for help and relief, your Body Talk will get louder and louder. The sooner you notice your Body Talk, the smaller the problem becomes and the easier it is to manage. When you ignore your Body Talk, problems magnify and can result in serious physical, mental or emotional consequences. Heart disease, some cancers, and stomach ulcers are only a few of the physical ailments that have ties to unresolved stress. Stress builds and does not go away until it is handled. Note that the overuse of unnecessary medications can mask stress and mute your Body Talk. Notice if you are self-medicating with recreational drugs, alcohol, over-the-counter medications or prescription pain medications. What is the Body Talk that you are attempting to silence?

Dreams can be another emotional form of Body Talk since you often work through issues from your daily life in your dreams. To use your dreams to explore your emotions, first notice when your dreams contain water because water is often an indicator of the emotions in your life. Next, notice the size of the body of water in your dream. Small bodies of water, like puddles or drips, usually indicate small, manageable emotions, while large, deep, or ominous bodies of water usually indicate unmanageable overwhelming feelings. When your dreams contain water, think about what emotions you might be experiencing in your daytime life. Do you remember from our discussion on self-worth that every one of your thoughts, feelings, and actions has meaning? Take that idea one step further: every one of the thoughts, feelings, and actions in your dreams has meaning in your daily life.

> Michele shared a dream about being on an island with a vast expanse of deep, dark water separating her from the mainland, where she could see other people in the distance. She recalled feeling isolated and fearful, overwhelmed by the task of getting off the island with no visible means of transportation. Michele realized that she was feeling overwhelmed at the prospect of delivering her second baby. The BIG feelings she associated with this event caused her to be emotionally isolated from her husband and even close family members (represented by the people in the distance in her dream) as the prospect of caring for two babies loomed closer and closer. Michele worked on seeing the upcoming birth in its right-size, and keeping her emotions in perspective. She knew she was not alone in meeting the demands of having two small children; she had a supportive husband and a caring, interested family. Recognizing that she was organized and ready for this challenge reduced the intensity and drama of the BIG feelings she was unconsciously attaching to it. Her dream helped her to recognize the BIG feelings she was experiencing, which allowed her to more easily handle the realities of the situation. This awareness helped Michele became grounded in the present.

Consider keeping a dream journal and working on associating events from your dreams to events in real time. Paying attention to your dreams is one way to tune into your body's messages and to obtain information about your stress and anxiety levels. We'll say more about dreams in A: Acceptance of the Whole and in E: Enjoy and Experience Life.

Your body is like a balloon that can hold just so much air. Just as too much air causes the balloon to burst, too much tension causes

Body Talk. When you don't attend to your body's needs, tension builds and Body Talk starts. Where do you hold your tension and anxiety in your body? How does your body communicate stress to you? Listen to your body. Be aware of what your body is telling you. Notice your Body Talk!

Charge Up Exercise Two
Listening to Your Body Talk!

Try the following body scan to become familiar with your personal body talk:

1. Find a place with few distractions and sit quietly in a chair or lie down for a few minutes. Take the time to notice your body. Do not judge anything that you become aware of. Simply notice each part of your body beginning from the top of your head and slowly moving down to the soles of your feet. As you do this, check for any negative feelings; for example, you may notice throbbing in your head, tension in your jaw, or butterflies in your stomach. Your body may be still holding **tension from your drive home or your hectic schedule. What is the message your body is sending you from each of these body parts?**

2. To relieve the negativity in your body, notice each part that feels tense, one by one, while taking several deep breaths. Focus on this body part and breathe into it until you notice the tension in it releasing. Practice this mini stress reliever and you'll find it works faster and faster each time to bring you closer to a state of calm. Notice how your body feels when it is comfortable and calm, because that is your goal.

3. Notice, for example, how your body feels when you finish a yoga class or a two-mile run. How does your body communicate the sensation of calm or energy to you? Do your muscles tingle? Do you have a broad smile on your face? Notice how your body communicates good feelings to you as well as warning signals.

H: Here and Now

Step Three: Keep Situations Right-Sized

Betty was being charged an extra fee by the airline for her bag that was over the weight limit. Betty couldn't believe the nerve of the airline to charge her, a frequent flyer, who she felt deserved a waiver on the fee. Betty became outraged and proceeded to rant and rave unleashing her anger on everyone around her. A manager intervened and suggested she switch a few items from the overweight bag to her carry-on, and quickly the problem was solved. Betty felt a bit embarrassed when she realized her anger was disproportionate to the situation. She had overreacted.

So far, in H: Here and Now, you learned that anxiety does not exist in the present, so the more time you spend in the present the less anxiety you will feel. Next, you learned to become aware of Body Talk, the physical signals your body sends to your mind to alert you to stress and anxiety. Now, consider how magnifying the importance of a situation causes anxiety when you don't keep things right-sized. When events are viewed as they truly are, right-sized, you move closer to being grounded in the present and, thus, better able to focus your energy on your goals and desires.

Perhaps you have experienced intense emotions at one time or another, such as great joy at the birth of a baby, or passionate grief at the loss of a loved one. These emotions are appropriate and fit the occasion. However, when events are magnified out of proportion to their importance, you can experience heightened emotions that we call BIG feelings. These reactions move you out of the present, where things are real, and into the past or future where old fears or apprehensions reside and can attempt to control you. These BIG feelings generate fear that the event you are dealing with could be the one that is the proverbial "straw that broke the camel's back," and this propels you into distress and worry. You feel panicked and out of control. Physical changes in your body limit your ability to think clearly and your emotions take over.

Some people experience BIG feelings more frequently than others do, and they bring these BIG feelings to most situations, even simple ones like making a decision about what to wear. These emotionally intense individuals might notice some type of Body Talk such as fatigue, headaches, muscle tension, difficulty swallowing, trembling, irritability, sweating, hot flashes, tension in the neck or shoulders, or butterflies in their stomachs, almost all the time. BIG feelings can be harmful when chronic overreactions lead to physical ailments such as heart attack or high blood pressure; being aware of them and having the perspective that fits is the key.

To begin to understand perspective, consider some of the worries and concerns you are having right now. Make a list of at least five or six of them and don't judge yourself for having them. Just allow yourself to express them. They can range from deciding which color to paint your bedroom or what to have for dinner all the way to which house you should buy or concerns about your health. Next, assign a worry rating to each item on your list using a scale from 1 to10, with 10 representing the most worried you could be about a situation and a 1 representing the least worried. For example, you might assign a worry rating of 6 to your car which has been making some strange noises and a worry rating of 8 to your child who has been running a fever of 101 degrees for two days. After you've rated each item, go back and assign a catastrophe rating to each item on your list, using a 1 to 10 rating scale once again, but now consider that a 10 represents the most catastrophic thing that you could ever imagine happening to you, and a 1 representing something that concerns you very little. Considering the previous examples, you might assign a catastrophe rating of 3 to the car because you know it can be fixed and a catastrophe rating of 4 to your child because you know her fever is a common reaction to a recent vaccine. Comparing your worry rating and your catastrophe rating should give you some idea of the true perspective of your worry. You'll see the true importance and severity of your worries, one by one. Are your ratings the same or different? If your ratings are the same, then you are probably good at keeping things in perspective and your worry ratings are realistic. If your worry ratings are higher than your catastrophe ratings by two or more, then your worries are magnified, and when you consider just how bad things could get, their intensity diminishes. The difference between ratings is the amount you have magnified them and attached BIG feelings to them.

Your daily life contains worries and concerns and you cannot eliminate them entirely nor should you try to. They are part of the human experience. Some anxiety keeps you safe and cognizant of the consequences of your behavior, but unmanaged anxiety is debilitating and can keep you from realizing your life goals and dreams. It is important to know how much anxiety you can handle, how to keep worries in perspective, and what to do about anxiety when you reach the point of feeling overwhelmed. This is the point when you stop feeling composed and competent and move into feeling overwhelmed. So consider how much cumulative anxiety is comfortable for you to manage at any one time before you cross the line and feel overwhelmed and out of control. How much can you handle before BIG feelings emerge and take over? Use a 1 to 10 rating with 1-3 representing an extremely low tolerance for worry, anxiety, and frustration, while 8-10 represents a very high tolerance for juggling many tasks simultaneously. A 4-7 rating means a moderate capacity for managing multiple problems and issues at home and work. Where do you fall on the scale? Label this number Cumulative Worry.

Some people can manage a level 5 of cumulative worry because they are **able to manage many things at once. Many can juggle a number of things with relative ease and still feel in control.** When they cross the line into a 6, however, they need to take a break or delegate some responsibility. Other people become overwhelmed at a 2. They manage low levels of anxiety well but generally need a calm, soothing, and relaxing environment to maintain control. How much anxiety can you handle? What is your comfort level? A higher rating is not better or more worthwhile than a lower rating. The rating only represents your individual capacity to manage worries and concerns and is not a value judgment. The only judgment to be made is an honest assessment of your needs. Know what your personal rating is and which signals indicate that you have exceeded it. As illustrated in the previous section, the amount of anxiety you can manage is like the amount of air that can fit in a balloon. Keep in mind that a balloon can accommodate just so much air before it bursts; the amount of additional air needed to pop a balloon can be quite small, depending upon how much air is already in the balloon.

The key is to keep the anxiety in your life, the air in your balloon manageable. Another way to do this is by using the 0 to 2 response check technique also described in the section Live In Your Circle of Integrity within G: Genuine and Authentic. When you express yourself by dealing with the issue at hand, you'll earn one point. For instance, say what you feel, express your opinion, make yourself visible in a respectful way, regardless of whether you receive the response you would like. Just expressing yourself keeps the amount of air in your balloon manageable. If, however, you earn zero points by stuffing your feelings, the air in your balloon expands and often a very minor incident is enough to create a BIG feeling that is out of proportion to the situation. That is when your balloon-of-anxiety pops. Reactions that are out of proportion to the situation signal that you have been holding in your feelings. Stuffed feelings can lead to physical ailments such as migraines, digestive problems, ulcers, and other illnesses. Work at expressing your feelings and you'll keep your emotions under control, just like the air in a balloon. Keeping a journal can be one way of expressing your feelings and earning a helpful point.

Recall the Body Talk you identified in the previous section, "Listen to Your Body Talk." With knowledge of Body Talk and an understanding of your capacity to manage worries and concerns that generate anxiety, you take the first step in keeping problems in your life right-sized. When you reach your breaking point, find ways to reduce your anxiety level to a manageable point. For example, if you have three projects running simultaneously at work and you recognize by the tension in your back that you are overwhelmed, you'll delegate one of the projects or look for assistance. Or, if you are the go-to-person for these three projects and no one else is available, you can think back to the information you learned about yourself in C: Compliment and Nurture. You can ask yourself, "What feels nurturing to me?" You might arrange for a relaxing massage after work or a quiet dinner with your spouse in a favorite restaurant. The key is to assess what you can handle, acknowledge your limitations, seek assistance and other means of self-support, and find ways to nurture yourself through it.

Keeping things right-sized is important because when anxiety-producing events pile up and you feel that you don't have the ability to handle them, tension builds, deadlines appear impossible and expectations insurmountable. When the anxiety the event generated is disproportionate to the actual event, you are unintentionally pulled out of the present and into the future, where anxiety lives. When events are kept in perspective, BIG feelings decrease and the solutions to problems become more visible to you.

Charge Up Exercise Three
Keeping Situations Right-Sized!

Try the following exercises to help keep your life more manageable:

1. Consider the times in your life when you reacted in a big way. For example, you may have yelled at your child, argued with a coworker, hung up the phone on a friend, or threw items across the room. Make a list of those Big reactions as shown below. Next, rate the level of your reaction on a scale of 1 to 10 with 10 being the most outrageous emotional reaction you could have expressed. Next, write down the event that initially triggered your reaction. Finally, rate on a scale of 1 to 10 the reaction that realistically fit that event. Write as many of your own examples as you can.

Reaction Displayed	Reaction Rating	Actual Event	Realistic Rating
Screamed at the top of my lungs at a coworker.	9	Coworker didn't remember to bring folding tables to our company event.	4

In the example above, an employee screamed uncontrollably (rating a 9) at a coworker who forgot to bring folding tables to a company event. Although the group needed the tables for the success of the event, in the grand scheme of life events, the realistic rating was a 4. A rating of 9 might be more appropriate to alert someone to danger, but doesn't fit when a coworker fails to bring an item to an event. Had the employee's reaction been right-sized, then solutions may have more readily emerged because she wouldn't have been swept away by her BIG feelings. This example shows a clearly disproportionate and catastrophic reaction to the actual event.

2. Make a list of actions you could take to prevent yourself from reacting to BIG feelings that don't match an event. For example, you could walk away from the situation, make sure you nurture your needs more often, or call a friend. What actions work best for you? Include in your list the situations listed in #1 and list a few ideas about what you could have done instead.

1. _____

2. _____

3. _____

4. _____

5. _____

6. _____

7. _____

8. _____

9. _____

H-Here and Now:

Step Four: Stay Grounded Through Your Senses

When Kelly met with her colleagues at work, she stayed focused on the conversation and the body language of others in the room during the meeting. She followed what was said and noticed the mannerisms of the participants. Kelly remained present by attending to what was actually before her. Staying grounded was about tuning in to and connecting with her colleagues in the moment.

Staying present helps you to realize your goals by reducing anxiety and increasing your feelings of control. Anxiety only occurs when you are distracted by thoughts of the past or the future; it doesn't exist in the present. It is impossible to be in two time dimensions at once, so when you function in the present, you feel focused and energized. But how do you stay grounded in the present? We've talked about several ways so far: First, get to know when you are not in the present. Understand at what point you are pulled into the past or the future. Next, listen to the signs of stress your body communicates to you. Also, when problems are viewed as manageable, the solutions to them are more readily apparent. Last but not least you'll learn to stay grounded in the present by using all your five senses.

Staying Grounded in the Present involves taking in information with all five senses by being aware of what is around you without judgment, bias, or attempts to direct and control. It is about experiencing and noticing what is versus what you want it to be. To remain grounded in the present and to know cognitively what is actually happening in your life right now, you must take in your current experience with all five senses: sight, sound, taste, touch, and smell. Staying grounded in the present is about allowing the world to be as it is, without judging it or exerting power over it. It is being aware of what is.

To become aware of what is, **your present reality**, try a sensory check-in, a valuable tool to use when you feel worried, concerned, or anxious. You can use it anytime and anywhere, and it will be most effective if you first practice using it and become familiar with it before you need it. Remember, fire drills aren't very effective in the middle of a fire, so practice the sensory check-in before you become stressed. You'll find that it will quickly bring on a state of calm when you need it.

Let's practice. Find a comfortable spot and sit or lie down. You will be practicing each one of the five senses, one by one. Say aloud or in your mind everything that you are experiencing bit by bit. First, let's work with sight. Choose something around you to focus on. It could be a picture on the wall, a shrub in the garden, or a piece of furniture, and describe it aloud. For example, "I see the lamp on my desk. It is small and has a curved light blue base and a white shade. The light hits the base at a variety of angles and makes shapes like stripes and circles, lighter and darker. The light gives a yellow tinge to the white shade which has a linen texture to it......." Get the idea? Now you try it with something you see. What do you notice about your body as you do this?

Next, let's focus on hearing. Say aloud all the sounds in your environment one by one. "I hear the hum of the air conditioner. I hear the sounds of the children's voices calling to one another outside. I hear the sound of my son talking on the phone. I hear the sound of a car as it passes by the house. I hear the hum of the refrigerator ..." Keep going until you have exhausted the list of possibilities associated with this sense. If you find it difficult to pay attention to this task, don't criticize or judge yourself. Just bring your mind back to the task and keep going.

Now let's try taste. What are the tastes in your mouth? Can you taste lunch or breakfast or your toothpaste, mouthwash, or breath mint? Are the tastes sweet, sharp, spicy, bitter, or salty? If no specific tastes are apparent, what does "no taste" taste like? Lick your lips and explore all the tastes in your mouth. Say them out loud.

Touch is next on the list and involves all the sensory experiences your skin is having at the moment. For example, "I feel the warm air on my cheeks and notice wisps of my hair as they move in the breeze. I feel my sandals on my feet and the firmness of the ground under my sandals. I feel the metallic weight of my necklace and the slight pinch of my earrings. I notice my T-shirt, is somewhat tight around my arms and loose and less noticeable around my trunk. I feel the rough linen texture of my pants and the weight of my body on the lawn chair. My arm rests on the glass top of the patio table and the metal rim feels cold." Now you describe all the sensations your skin is feeling at this moment, out loud.

Finally, we end with smell. What do you smell in the air? Foods, scents, paint, cleaning products? Is the dander of your cat or dog in the air? The smell of fish at the beach? The scent of flowers in the garden? Your neighbor barbecuing? What is the range of scents that are available to you at this very moment? Say them aloud, one by one. Breathe them in.

When you do the sensory check-in you'll create a feeling of relaxation. Your breaths become longer and you might even sigh, Ah-hhh. Wherever you hold tension in your body, you'll feel it release. Wherever you have held stress in your body, you'll notice a change. In workshops, we've noticed individuals taking deep, cleansing breaths, releasing the tightness in their faces, or letting go of the tension in their shoulders as their minds become aware of the present.

Keep trying and you will notice your attention span and ability to reach a state of calm increase. As you practice this technique you will need only seconds to reduce your anxiety and ground yourself in the present. The ideal time to practice this exercise is when you are feeling calm so that when you are in a stressful situation, you are able to perform the technique more easily. Individuals who suffer from performance anxiety find it especially helpful to use the sensory check-in.

Morgan becomes especially anxious before tests. When her teachers places the paper before her, she leaps into the future and imagines that the test has been graded and she's failed, all before she's responded to the first question. Her anxiety prevents her from recalling information that she knows and seems to freeze her brain. She consistently underperforms, which fuels her sense of inadequacy. By using the sensory check-in, Morgan has been able to stay present with the test at the time she is taking it. When she feels but-

terflies in her stomach, her personal body talk, she stops and chooses a sense to focus on. Within seconds she feels calmer and returns to the test, better able to recall the information she has studied so hard to learn.

When you have become experienced at the sensory check-in, you can use it in a variety of circumstances, such as when you find it difficult to fall asleep. If your body needs rest, doing the sensory check-in will allow you to drift to sleep in minutes rather than lying awake and tossing and turning. As you lie in bed, say what you are experiencing with each of your senses. If the room is very dark, avoid sight because straining to see something may stimulate you rather than relax you. Say something like: "I am lying in my bed and I feel the breeze of the fan on my face. My feet feel the soft sheets, and my body is aware of the light pressure of the sheet and blanket. My head rests on my pillow ..." Get it? Try the sensory check-in whenever you sense body talk, if you are anxious before a social meeting or a delayed flight, or when you are frustrated by a snag in traffic. At first, it may be difficult to sustain attention for even seconds without your mind wandering. This is normal unless you are an experienced meditator. Be patient and kind to yourself, and watch your stress level diminish.

Being present in your life allows you to take the most enjoyment from what you do. Our culture is fast-paced and filled with expectations about where you "should" be and what you "should" accomplish. But literally, the only place you can be is where you are. It's impossible to be in two places at once. You lose your life minute by minute ... hour by hour ... by allowing anxiety about where you're not and what you're not doing to override your enjoyment of the present. Have you ever talked to a friend on the phone while you were checking your calendar or making a grocery list? Did you end the call and wonder what you talked about because you missed most of it by trying to do two things at once? It's impossible to be in two places at once, and the only place you can be is in the present. Enjoy where you are! Allow prudence and restraint to have a place in your life. Consider that where you are at this moment is right. Do a sensory check-in to notice your surroundings and fully experience them. Take a calm, decisive interest in determining comfortable limits for yourself, rather than continuously focusing on stretching yourself, to the limits of your strength and endurance. Be present with your life!

Charge Up Exercise Four
Stay Grounded Through Your Senses!

Practice noticing your world with the following:

1. Try using your five senses when eating a meal: sight, sound, taste, touch, and smell. Take the time to enjoy the smells coming from the food before you. Notice the shapes, textures, and colors of the foods you are eating. Savor each bite, noticing the feel of the food in your mouth and the flavors on your tongue. Is it crunchy or soft? Be aware of how the food makes you feel as it enters your body. Was it satisfying to you? Did it feel nourishing and pleasurable, or did it cause discomfort in any way?

2. Notice your immediate environment as you go to work or as you go about your day. Notice and breathe in the colors and textures of the world around you. Notice the sounds around you. What's different today? Experience the subtleties of life. Connect, experience, enjoy!

3. Take the time to connect with your present world by making a list of the things you notice right now through your five senses. Make a note of what it feels like to orient yourself to your world in this way. When you are experiencing life in the present by tuning into your five senses, you are free from anxiety and ready to charge forward.

Charge Up Your Life Milestones

H: Here and Now

Now that you have finished H: Here and Now, what skills have you learned and what ones are you still working on?

- Put a check mark in front of the statements that feel true to you right now.
- Put a circle in front of the statements that you have not yet achieved.

____ I practice staying present with my life.

____ I review situations from the past but don't ruminate on perceived failures.

____ I plan for the future but don't worry about it.

____ I believe I can handle whatever happens.

____ My body talks to me through physical complaints, and I listen.

____ I know how to manage my anxiety.

____ I pay attention to the messages in my dreams that contain water.

____ I deal with reality and avoid making up stories that keep me stuck.

____ An awareness of my five senses keeps me grounded in the here and now.

____ I understand what triggers me and makes me anxious.

_____ I practice the O-2 Response Check by earning one point whenever possible.

_____ I let go of what isn't working for me anymore without judging myself a failure.

_____ I use techniques that help me stay present and focused.

_____ I'm working on using "H: Here and Now" in the following ways:

_____

_____

_____

_____

_____

_____

_____

_____

_____

_____

_____

_____

_____

_____

_____

_____

H – Here and Now

Additional Resources

The following is a list of suggested materials to help you on your journey to managing stress and anxiety:

- *The Grief Recovery Handbook* by John W. James and Russell Friedman – a step-by-step guide to dealing with loss.

- *Taming Your Gremlin: a surprisingly simple method for getting out of your own way* by Rick Carlson – practice being in the here and now by noticing, listening, choosing, and banishing the gremlin within.

- *Practicing the Power of Now: Essential Teachings, Meditations, and Exercises from the Power of Now* by Eckhart Tolle – a short and easy to follow spiritual guide to a transformation of human consciousness and enlightenment.

- *Five Good Minutes: 100 morning practices to help you stay calm and focused all day long* by Jeffrey Brantley, M.D. and Wendy Millstine - daily exercises to reduce stress and keep you centered.

- *A Year by the Sea* by Joan Anderson – one woman's journey of self-discovery.

"Breathe. Let go.
And remind yourself
that this very moment
is the only one
you know you have
for sure."

—Joan Didion,
Oprah Magazine, May 2004

Accept Your Possibilities

Self-Limiting Beliefs ◄————► Unlimited Possibilities

- Notice Every Trait
- Be Proud of Your Anchors
- Understand Your Triggers
- Use All Your Traits

"Value every part of you."

"All of us have the potential
to embody
all manner of human qualities...
We encompass all possible
human dimensions and polarities
although we may not be
in touch with them."

—Jennifer Mackewn,
psychotherapist, writer

A: Accept Your Possibilities
Self-Limiting Beliefs ◄──────► Unlimited Possibilities

Introduction

Loretta felt lost after her youngest child left home for college. Being a mom was a big part of her identity. What was she going to do with her time if she wasn't managing her child's schedule, juggling cars, planning meals, and being available for support and nurturance? Loretta had long ago lost touch with who she was and what she personally aspired to in her life. She couldn't remember what she liked to do or what made her happy, other than being a devoted mom. Loretta decided to start a new chapter in her life. She began a journey of self-discovery, exploring new ideas and interests along with uncovering her long forgotten traits and talents.

Recognizing, accepting, and valuing every personal trait is important in order to realize your potential. When you define yourself in a narrow way, by using only a small number of traits, you limit yourself and the possibilities for your life. For example, in a very broad sense, if you see yourself as an athlete, you might have a hard time also seeing yourself as a scholar. You might be missing out on developing your intellect because you are over-defining yourself or limiting yourself, by your athletic ability. You minimize the one trait, intelligence, and over-emphasize the other trait, athleticism. Or, think of young women who are very attractive and get "stuck on pretty" in defining themselves. They often experience great dismay as they age and find that they have over-identified their self-worth by their looks, and as a result they fail to develop their other qualities, such as sociability, intellect, and generosity. In truth, you have the ability to access all traits and you enrich yourself and expand on the possibilities for your life by developing the whole of you.

In A: Accept Your Possibilities, you will learn the four components that help you reach your full potential. Moving through them is necessary in order to live your life to the fullest. In this section you will learn that you have access to many traits and that all traits have value. In addition, you will discover the importance of understanding anchors, the traits you most value, and triggers, the traits that cause you to feel shame. Also, you'll explore the power of shame and guilt and the role each plays in creating self-doubt and self-distrust, which can hold you back from being the winning person you want to be. Knowing that there is a time and a place for all of your traits helps you understand their usefulness and value and helps you to work on developing your "whole" by finding the right fit for all of your traits. Then you can realize your potential, increase your self-confidence, and work on becoming the best you can be.

A
Famous Person Experience

Think of a famous person in any industry, from politics, to Hollywood, to social causes, any person that you would characterize as famous or newsworthy, without judging the person that comes to your mind.

Next, think of that person's traits and qualities, talents and strengths, weaknesses and quirks. What do you notice about them? What is he known for? What do you admire in her? What annoys you about him? Make a list of your famous person's positive and negative qualities. Try to come up with at least five to ten of each, even if you have to use your imagination a bit to identify what these positive and negative traits might be. Label the positive qualities you have identified anchors, and label the negative qualities, at least five to ten of each. Label the positive qualities "anchors" and the negative qualities "triggers."

Consider the list of anchors. Do you have these positive qualities? Would you like to have them? These traits are meaningful to you in some way. You may notice people being praised for having them or you may have been praised when you did.

Now, consider the list of triggers. Do you have these negative qualities? Are you proud of them? Are you ashamed of them? Have you been criticized for displaying them? Do you wish you had them? These traits are also meaningful to you in some way. They represent challenges you face in your life.

This activity shows you that everthing you notice in someone else says something about you. You notice what you value and what you are challenged by. Try this with other famous people and you'll discover more about yourself.

A: Accept Your Possibilities

Step One: Notice Every Trait

Kitty was a contradiction. She was a conscientious, responsible, and highly valued, employee who was meticulous and detail-oriented about her work as a medical researcher. However, Kitty was also a fun-loving and freedom-seeking young woman who valued independence and spontaneity. She loved to travel because it allowed her to meet new people and explore new places. She often felt as if she needed to continually decide between honoring her need for security and honoring her need for adventure. Kitty needed to find a way to honor all her traits. Many people are like Kitty, a combination of seemingly disparate traits, which together create a very unique individual.

Traits are enduring personality characteristics that describe you, such as sensitive, kind, generous, critical, assertive, frugal. Think of how you would describe yourself. For example, if you consider yourself to be a serious and logical person, then you approach situations with a rational and data-based mind set. If, however, you consider yourself to be curious and open-minded, you approach situations with many questions and look for options and choices. The traits which you feel embody your **personality provide stability, and balance.** They reinforce to you who you are; they are your personal identity markers.

Take a look at the Trait Box that follows. In addition to the traits that you identify with easily, you can actually use every trait in this box. As a whole person, you have access to a complete array of personality traits and when you can see all traits in yourself, you enrich your identity and expand on the possibilities for your life. You begin to see yourself as a "whole" human. But when you define yourself in a narrow way, using a limited list of traits, you restrict the possibilities in your life.

Trait Box

Active, adaptable, adventurous, affectionate, afraid, aggressive, aloof, analytical, apathetic, artistic, assertive, athletic, attentive, astute, attractive, awkward, bad, bashful, bitter, bold, brave, calm, carefree, caring, cautious, charitable, cheerful, childish, compassionate, collaborative, competent, competitive, concerned, condescending, confident, confrontational, congenial, considerate, creative, critical, curious, daring, decisive, dedicated, dependent, depressed, detached, determined, devious, devoted, dexterous, diplomatic, direct, discreet, dull, dynamic, eager, easygoing, effective, emotional, empathic, energetic, enthusiastic, extroverted, faithful, fearful, fearless, firm, flexible, foresighted, forgetful, forgiving, friendly, frivolous, fun-loving, generous, giving, grumpy, gullible, happy, hateful, headstrong, healthy, hedonistic, hesitant, hopeful, honest, humble, humorous, idealistic, ignorant, important, impractical, impulsive, inadequate, inferior, inquisitive, insecure, insensitive, intellectual, intense, intrigued, introverted, involved, jealous, jolly, jovial, judgmental, just, kind, knowledgeable, lazy, liberated, light-hearted, liked, logical, lonely, lovable, loving, magnanimous, mean, meek, moody, motivated, naïve, nasty, needy, negative, neglected, nervous, odd, old, open-minded, opinionated, organized, outgoing, pampered, passionate, passive, patient, pensive, perceptive, persistent, persuasive, playful, poor, positive, powerless, practical, quiet, rambunctious, rational, rebellious, reluctant, respectful, responsible, rigid, sad, self-centered, sedentary, selfish, sensible, serious, sophisticated, spontaneous, spunky, stingy, strong, stubborn, subservient, talented, talkative, tenacious, tender, thoughtful, thoughtless, tolerant, tranquil, trusted, truthful, ugly, uncaring, understanding, uptight, vain, vicious, vigilant, vulnerable, whimsical, witty.

Although you have access to every trait, typically you have a small number of traits you believe define you and distinguish you from others around you. This group of traits is often referred to as your "identity." You were born with some of these traits and acquired others as you matured. Identity formation is a process that occurs over a lifetime.

Some of the traits you embody are determined by your temperament, such as adaptability to change, your general need for physical activity, **your** ability to tolerate frustration before you react, the intensity of your reactions, the general quality of your mood (either positive or negative), and the amount of persistence that you are able to display.

If you asked your parents or siblings to rate you on these elements of temperament, they would probably tell you that they've noticed the same level of these qualities in you since birth. That is the general view of temperament: you were born with a certain temperament that is generally resistant to change. So, your mother might tell you that you were very adaptable and didn't eat on a rigid schedule; that you were a quiet baby who enjoyed being held for long periods, but that you were tolerant of being left in your crib with toys while she managed the household and your older siblings. She also might tell you that you had a generally positive mood but that when you had enough of waiting for her attention you displayed an intense reaction and didn't stop until your specific need for food, changing, or cuddling was met. In addition, your mom might say you had a long attention span and even at a very young age, could focus on putting together a puzzle long after your peers had moved on to another activity. So, all of these examples give you a fair idea of the temperament you were born with. You can determine whether these same traits are visible in your adult life.

Next, you could ask yourself whether you honor your very unique temperament and allow yourself to nurture those traits that brought you feelings of comfort and pleasure as a young child. For example, if you are an individual with low persistence, you like to change activities after a specific period of time: maybe fifteen minutes, or maybe an hour. Whatever the time, you have an internal clock that signals to you how long you can continue with an activity before getting distracted from it by either environmental stimulation or internal body talk. Do you insist that you complete a task totally before you move on, or do you honor your internal clock and take a brief break and come back to it? Were you aware that your temperament was responsible for this trait? Are you able to accept, love, and not judge this trait as better or worse than another trait?

Traits are also shaped by your environment because the people you interact with value some traits and devalue others. The active and talkative child learns to sit quietly in church, synagogue, or mosque, because the cost of being more active, no dessert after dinner or an early bedtime, is too high a price to pay. Your school experiences also shape you because teachers and administrators value very specific behaviors in the school setting, such as listening, paying attention, and following rules.

Have you read the book *All I Really Need to Know I Learned in Kindergarten* by Robert Fulghum? He talks about some of these very important social behaviors that you learn when you first begin school. They can develop into enduring traits such as punctuality, responsibility, and sociability, which you carry with you into the workplace as an adult where these traits continue to be reinforced and shaped.

In adolescence, identity development is at a peak. Do you remember the trials and tribulations of being an early teen? Your main goals were probably to fit in, to be liked, and to avoid criticism, but underlying these was the intention of finding out about you. Teens separate emotionally from parents sometimes by disagreeing with whatever an adult says; by trying out new hairstyles, new groups of friends, or new manners of dress; or by speaking and acting in different ways to see what the reaction will be. If the reaction, shock or approval, was the one you wanted, you probably stuck with the behavior, but if it elicited a reaction you weren't counting on you probably dropped the behavior ... fast. Social, family, and work relationships continue to form, shape, and modify your identity as you mature.

As adults, your traits identify you to your family, friends, coworkers, and acquaintances; although you have access to every trait in the trait box, other people reinforce some and not others.

Ethan's close friends knew him as fun-loving, witty, and talkative. They often invited him to parties and other social occasions because he was lively and sociable. These socially desirable qualities defined one aspect of

Ethan's personality, and were reinforced by his friends. Some traits, however, are less socially desirable and carry a negative connotation with them such as being critical or judgmental. For example, Tina's analytical mind was razor sharp at homing in on missed details and inconsistencies in portfolios, and she was clear and direct in communicating her findings. Yet her coworkers hurt her feelings with comments such as, "You're so critical!" These comments caused her to decline opportunities to use her outstanding analytical skills and she kept her comments to herself. Consider that Tina's coworkers could have looked at her skills in a more positive light.

In the example above, the trait "critical" became "analytical," which completely changed the view of the trait. The trait became quite marketable and desirable. Simply change the tone of the word, but not the actual behavior, and the judgment is removed. This may help you to more easily recognize that you have access to every trait. Some traits that you may view as negative also have a positive view.

Dreamwork is another way to increase your awareness of the traits that compose your identity. In dreams, houses represent your view of yourself. So, if your dreams contain houses, think of how you would describe each house: beautiful, stately, run-down, in a state of disrepair, bright, cheerful, well lighted, polished, or well cared for. Chances are those same descriptors are ones that you could apply to yourself at the time of the dream. For example, if you are taking on too many tasks at work and feeling tired and run down, your dream might contain a house that is literally falling apart, and you might see yourself as inadequate or insecure. If you are in love and feeling cherished and cared for, your dream might contain a house that is the showpiece of the neighborhood with spacious rooms, many windows and beautiful furniture. Thus, you might see yourself as lovable and positive. Keep in mind that all representations of objects in dreams are products of your own personal filter. If your idea of a beautiful home is a cabin in the woods, then that is how you will represent a positive identity in your dream. If the previous description of the "showpiece" house communicates arrogance or wastefulness then that is how you are feeling about yourself when you dream about it. Add to the dream journal you started in H—Here and Now by noticing the houses in your dreams and see what insight this can give you about how you are feeling about yourself. What traits are you using to define yourself in your dreams?

So far, we've talked about traits that you recognize in yourself, ones that you easily identify with. They are the ones that most people see in you and count on you to display. If you own a trait you believe represents you, you most likely will have difficulty owning the opposite trait.

> *Emma was a generous young woman who gave freely of her time, as well as her money, to a local charity. She could identify with the trait "generous" but could not easily see herself as "stingy." After some thought, she discovered that she could be stingy, such as when she would refuse to tip a waiter who did not offer excellent service. Emma had both traits and so do you.*

Using the example above, think of a time you've been "generous" and a time you've been "stingy." Or, perhaps you chose "sensible" as one of the traits you identified with and saw as one of your core traits. You are a sensible individual and you solve problems using logic and reason. But aren't you also frivolous and adventurous at times? Can you think of a time when you were frivolous or adventurous, when you did not choose the sensible course of action?

You have every trait because you are a whole person. For example, if you can be serious, you can also be light-hearted. You may express some traits more often than others but a lesser frequency does not negate the presence or the importance of the trait. Frequency is not associated with importance. A trait you express less frequently may be a true marker of your uniqueness.

> *Sheila was generally known for being easygoing and adaptable because she was typically eager to adapt to avoid conflict. On occasion, however, she was quite opinionated, especially on the topic of animal rights. Her friends knew of her interest in animals but were still surprised when quiet Sheila expressed her opinions about them with such fervor. Sheila was capable of being easygoing as well as opinionated. She had both traits because she was a whole person. You are, too!*

The above example illustrates that you have the power to express all traits because you are a whole and complete person.

Charge Up Exercise One
Notice Every Trait!

1. Look at the traits below and see how each one fits you. Imagine yourself displaying each of the listed traits. Is each trait one you can easily identify with or does it feel strange or uncomfortable to you? Think of a time when you displayed each trait. Jot down that experience next to each trait below.

Trait	Experience
Witty	I was witty when I shared a joke and won a contest at a comedy club.
Extroverted	I was extroverted when …
Lazy	I was lazy when …
Frivolous	I was frivolous when …
Self-centered	I was self-centered when …
Persuasive	I was persuasive when …
Critical	I was critical when …
Kind	I was kind when …
Vulnerable	I was vulnerable when …

Stubborn	I was stubbormn when...
Dynamic	I was dynamic when...
Generous	I was generous when...
Thoughtless	I was thoughtless when...

2. In the box below, we've taken a few traits from the previous list and flipped them to their opposites. See if you can own these traits as well. Consider a time or times when you have exhibited these opposing traits. Even if you can't completely own these traits as markers of your personality, think of a time when you exhibited each of them. When was that? What were the circumstances? This can be difficult because you may tend to see yourself in either-or terms.

Trait	Experience
Dull	I identified with being dull when I was at a party surrounded by people having a great time together and I just couldn't find a way to fit in.
Introverted	I identified with being introverted when...
Energetic	I identified with being energetic when...
Serious	I identified with being serious when...
Selfless	I identified with being selfless when I...
Unconvincing	I identified with being unconvincing when...

3. As a challenge, look over the traits listed in the Trait Box once again and see if you can think of a time when you displayed each one of them. Don't judge yourself for being selfish, rigid, demanding, critical, and so on. Just allow yourself to see that you are capable of displaying each and every trait. Then, flip each trait and think of a time when you displayed that opposite trait. Notice the ones which are difficult to own.

These exercises will broaden your view of your personal identity. You will no longer view yourself using a finite set of traits but will see that you have the ability to exhibit any trait. You have the freedom to express any trait. Recognize that you are a whole person and has every trait. Start noticing the traits you have difficulty identifying with. Try them out. Try them on. Experiment with them. Notice what it feels like. Finding love, happiness, and success involves seeing that you are a whole person with access to every trait.

A: Accept Your Possibilities

Step Two: Be Proud of Your Anchors

Brooke was cautious about making decisions because she felt she made better decisions after more thought. Brooke saw "caution" as being an Anchor for her and, when she was cautious, she felt grounded and confident. When her colleagues noticed her making thoughtful business decisions, she felt proud. This feeling of pride caused her to identify even more strongly with caution as a personal Anchor.

You have every trait. This means that at one time or another you have probably exhibited every trait listed in the Trait Box. This is because you are a whole person and you have the ability to display any and every trait. You aren't confined to a finite set of traits or behaviors. There are traits, however, which you easily identify with and feel pride in and we refer to these traits as Anchors. Anchors are comfortable for you to express because they are in sync with your personality and temperament. They are likely to have been reinforced in your early experiences with family, teachers, and friends. Thus, the child who is active and physical may develop "energetic" as an Anchor because he not only requires a high level of physical activity, but that trait was also reinforced within his athletic family.

The traits you are most proud of are like the Anchors of a ship; they ground you and define you in ways that make you feel valued. You feel good when people notice them and praise you for them. Anchors are strengthened through your social interactions.

You are most comfortable when you place yourselves in situations where your Anchors are valued. Self-nurturing, which was discussed in C—Compliment and Nurture is involved. You feel nurtured when you are happy; you nurture yourself when you support your need to display your Anchors. For example, an individual who has an artistic temperament is not apt to be happy at a desk job working with numbers and business ledgers. Neither is an in-

Trait Box

Active, adaptable, adventurous, affectionate, afraid, aggressive, aloof, analytical, apathetic, artistic, assertive, athletic, attentive, astute, attractive, awkward, bad, bashful, bitter, bold, brave, calm, carefree, caring, cautious, charitable, cheerful, childish, compassionate, collaborative, competent, competitive, concerned, condescending, confident, confrontational, congenial, considerate, creative, critical, curious, daring, decisive, dedicated, dependent, depressed, detached, determined, devious, devoted, dexterous, diplomatic, direct, discreet, dull, dynamic, eager, easygoing, effective, emotional, empathic, energetic, enthusiastic, extroverted, faithful, fearful, fearless, firm, flexible, foresighted, forgetful, forgiving, friendly, frivolous, fun-loving, generous, giving, grumpy, gullible, happy, hateful, headstrong, healthy, hedonistic, hesitant, hopeful, honest, humble, humorous, idealistic, ignorant, important, impractical, impulsive, inadequate, inferior, inquisitive, insecure, insensitive, intellectual, intense, intrigued, introverted, involved, jealous, jolly, jovial, judgmental, just, kind, knowledgeable, lazy, liberated, light-hearted, liked, logical, lonely, lovable, loving, magnanimous, mean, meek, moody, motivated, naïve, nasty, needy, negative, neglected, nervous, odd, old, open-minded, opinionated, organized, outgoing, pampered, passionate, passive, patient, pensive, perceptive, persistent, persuasive, playful, poor, positive, powerless, practical, quiet, rambunctious, rational, rebellious, reluctant, respectful, responsible, rigid, sad, self-centered, sedentary, selfish, sensible, serious, sophisticated, spontaneous, spunky, stingy, strong, stubborn, subservient, talented, talkative, tenacious, tender, thoughtful, thoughtless, tolerant, tranquil, trusted, truthful, ugly, uncaring, understanding, uptight, vain, vicious, vigilant, vulnerable, whimsical, witty.

dividual who is extroverted apt to choose to work at home or to pursue a career as an accountant, since broad social contact in each would be limited. The creativity of the artist and the sociability of the extrovert need expression in order for these individuals to feel nurtured and valued.

You also notice people who display your Anchors. Sometimes you are attracted to them and sometimes you are repelled by them but, at all times, you are aware of them. Everything you think, say, and do is about you and everything you notice is also all about you.

> Luke was sophisticated and he enjoyed being around others who shared his interests in the arts, fine food, and expensive clothes. Sophistication was one of his Anchors and he enjoyed the camaraderie of others who were sophisticated as well. Luke appreciated others who shared his Anchor. Ian, however, was opinionated and vocal about his thoughts on most subjects. He liked being the center of attention when he good-naturedly expounded on his views. He noticed when others were also opinionated and vocal but did not appreciate this quality in them. He resented their infringement on his perceived territory, disliked debating points he felt were self-evident, and preferred that others defer to him or offer grudging acceptance of his views. He looked upon being opinionated as an Anchor for him but did not see it positively in others.

It is most likely easy for you to identify your Anchors and comfortable for you to express them but Anchors are not always helpful. Sometimes they can be your Achilles' heels by limiting your personal growth.

> Aaron was known as easygoing and adaptable. He had been praised for these traits all his life; they were in sync with his laid back temperament and he saw them as Anchors because they worked for him in most situations. However, they became a problem when dealing with his parents over his career choice. They had planned on having him follow his father into the family corporate law firm. Privately, however, Aaron felt the study of law was boring and mundane. Aaron had a dilemma before him. Staying with his Anchors, being conciliatory and appeasing, would not be helpful in this situation if Aaron wanted to make his own career choice. Aaron's

strength became his Achilles Heel. He would need to tap into other traits, such as being opinionated and decisive, in order to prevail in a conversation with his parents about their expectations for his future. He needed to recognize the limitations of his Anchors

Charge Up Exercise Two
Be Proud of Your Anchors!

Explore your Anchors in the following ways:

1. Look over the traits listed in the Trait Box, choose the ones
    that you feel most strongly define you as a person, and write
    them in the spaces below. Remember, Anchors ground you
    and define you in ways that make you feel comfortable and
    valued.

_____   _____

_____   _____

_____   _____

2. Look over your choices and note how you express them in
    your daily life. Notice how they are reinforced in your en-
    vironment by family, friends, or coworkers.

_____

_____

3. In what ways were your Anchors shaped and reinforced in
    your early life by adults such as parents, extended family
    members, or teachers?

_____

_____

A: Accept Your Possibilities

Step Three: Understand Your Triggers

> Joyce's mother criticized her for being assertive as a young child. Joyce's childlike need for independence was threatening to her mother's need to control her. This led to feelings of shame, even as an adult, when Joyce tried to be assertive in the workplace and in her marriage. To avoid these feelings of shame, assertiveness became a trait that Joyce tried to repress. This diminished her effectiveness at work since she avoided giving opinions and, when she did, she criticized herself and ruminated over her words. Assertiveness became a Trigger for Joyce, a button that could be easily, and often unwittingly, pushed by others. Joyce felt bad about being assertive; she felt ashamed even if her assertive behavior was being praised. She couldn't enjoy the compliment because it unconsciously generated shame for her.

Shame is often paired with Guilt. Some of your traits make you feel defensive or ashamed, and have the potential to create conflict. These traits are "Triggers," buttons in you that others push, often unknowingly and unintentionally. You try not to express them, but when you do, you feel guilt and shame. Shame is an emotion that occurs when you buy into someone else's negative or judged opinion of you causing you to feel wrong, undeserving, and worthless. Shame makes you feel that you don't deserve your hopes and dreams. Shame is often paired with Guilt, but the two have a subtle difference. Guilty feelings occur when you believe you did something wrong. It is the person's action that is judged. When little Stephanie, for example, took a cookie from the cookie jar she felt "guilty," because she believed she did something wrong. Shame, however, is generally a stronger and deeper emotion. It implies there is something wrong with you internally which causes you to turn inward and criticize that part of you. If you **feel ashamed, you feel** you are wrong at your essence, and your self-worth erodes just a bit. For example, when Stephanie's mother discovered her eating a cookie just before dinner she told Stephanie that she was bad because she "never" listens. Stephanie felt ashamed of her headstrong trait which often created conflict with her mother.

When you **take these negative associations to specific traits with you into adulthood, they act as Triggers of Guilt and Shame. You are not proud of these traits and, if you think back into the past, you may find that you have been criticized for expressing them.**

The effects of shame can range from mild to horribly damaging. Deep feelings of shame can lead to suicide, raging anger, or painful shyness—some people can't move past these negative feelings and the effects follow them throughout their lives. Understanding how shame is holding you back is the key to unlocking your full potential and living the life you want.

Dana recalled dressing for a high school dance and as she preened in front of the mirror she worried aloud about whether her outfit looked good enough and whether she should change. Her mother overheard her and remarked, "Who's going to look at You!" Dana immediately felt shamed and since she valued her mother's opinion, the event planted a seed of doubt about her personal appearance which grew even though she matured into an attractive young woman. Pride in her appearance became an area of shame for Dana and created deep feelings of insecurity in her. At times, she literally had difficulty "showing her face" without feeling shamed. When she spoke with others she often felt self-conscious about her appearance and worried that they might find her unattractive. She often interpreted positive remarks about her appearance as condescending and untruthful. She couldn't accept the praise.

Words such as "should," "have to," "always," and "never" and judgments such as "good," bad," "right," or "wrong" can be used to control you at different times in your life. For example, a parent may scold a child for "never listening," a friend may criticize you as "always being late," or a spouse may state that you "shouldn't get angry." When important people in your life use these words to direct or limit your behavior, **it generates** feelings of anger, fear, or sadness in you. You do not feel happy when you have disappointed someone whom you love or want to be appreciated by, and these negative feelings about the traits you are expressing often develop into Triggers. These Triggers unconsciously shape your behavior in the future and can cause you to feel shamed when you express them.

Triggers can also develop throughout your adult life when people who are important to you, such as family, friends, or coworkers, subtly or directly criticize you for the way you express yourself.

> Dorie's close friend was constantly telling her how her clothes looked dowdy and her home furnishings were outdated. Dorie understood that her friend meant well and that she was encouraging Dorie to update and get trendy, but her friend's manner of speaking was blunt and her words stung. Dorie's confidence about fashion and design was undermined by her friend's comments. Dorie reacted by doubting her sense of style and fashion. She avoided socializing in her home, and felt powerless to do anything about it. Dorie felt shamed and lost confidence in her ability to decorate her home. She gave up because she allowed her friend to plant a seed of shame in her mind.

Guilt and shame can be the cause of personal issues such as perfectionism, procrastination, compulsions, addictions, low aspirations, and general unhappiness. All can hold you back from realizing your dreams. These dysfunctional behaviors are ways you avoid coming in contact with the guilt and shame of your personal triggers and they are created when you absorb someone else's negative or judgmental opinion of you.

> Chad was a perfectionist in his home, work, and personal relationships. He developed these unrealistic expectations in his childhood when his best efforts were frequently judged as inadequate. Chad was a gifted learner who was chastised for the things he didn't excel at. He was often told he "should" do better in these areas, rather than being praised for the things he did do well. Thus, he developed into a perfectionist, criticizing his best efforts at everything.

You continue the cycle of guilt and shame when you judge yourself and others. You judge others when they display one of your personal Triggers. There may be nothing wrong with that trait, but shame was generated when you were criticized for expressing it. From our earlier examples, Joyce became critical of "assertive" people, Chad frequently judged his children and coworkers as "inadequate" and Dana found flaws in the most attractive super model or movie star. Notice what traits you find annoying in others. They say something about you because everything you think, feel, and do is ultimately about you. For example, if you are quiet and shy socially, you may notice individuals who socialize easily, perhaps because you wish you had more of that trait. Or, if you are impulsive and outspoken you may notice individuals who are controlled and calm because you secretly wish you could be more laid back and less reactive.

Sometimes you can recognize your triggers by the traits you envy in others. You judge in others the traits that you envy in them, the traits you yearn for, the traits you feel shame over or the traits you feel afraid of expressing. Shame and guilt are diminished when you understand how the cycle works, when you accept all parts of yourself, and take pride in being who you are. You own all of your parts and take pride and delight in having all of them. You own your previously disowned parts and move towards becoming complete and whole.

Charge Up Exercise Three
Understand Your Triggers!

Obtain a better understanding of what triggers you by completing the following:

1. Fill in the statements below to help you identify your "Triggers." Remember, Triggers are the traits that make you feel defensive or ashamed and are buttons that others push in you, even unknowingly and unintentionally.

* I should always remember to_____
  _____
  _____

* People get angry with me when I'm _____
  _____
  _____

* One thing I really need to change about _____
  _____
  _____

* I hate myself when I'm_____
  _____.
  _____

* I should never forget to be_____
  _____
  _____

2. Another way to identify your Triggers is to look at the flip side or opposite of your Anchors. Often, just recognizing and being aware of your Triggers helps deflate them, and you begin to see them for what they are. List your Anchors below, then flip them by listing their opposites to find your Triggers.

Your Anchors	Your Triggers
_____	_____
_____	_____
_____	_____
_____	_____
_____	_____
_____	_____
_____	_____
_____	_____
_____	_____

A: Accept Your Possibilities

Step Four: Use All of Your Traits

Coreen took pride in being dependable and considered it to be one of her Anchors. She could be counted on in her work as a copywriter to have her projects in by their deadlines, to arrive at work on time, and to collaborate cheerfully with others. Coreen could be counted on to help out wherever there was a need. Being dependable, however, worked against Coreen when her coworkers volunteered her to make all of the arrangements for an upcoming office social event. Her coworkers never checked this out with her and Coreen felt taken advantage of. Being dependable was an asset in many situations for Coreen but not in all situations. Coreen needed to adjust her view of herself as a dependable person. Her Anchor could be a weakness and a challenge for her depending upon when she chose to use it.

You have many traits and each trait has value. A trait can be an Anchor or a Trigger depending on your past experiences with it. The final lesson in accepting your possibilities is to understand that every trait has a place, and that you have access to every trait. A trait can work for you or against you depending on when and how it is used. For example, it is likely that if you take pride in being "witty," and consider it to be one of your Anchors, you can think of a time when it was an asset for you, such as at a cocktail party. However, you can probably also think of a time when it did not work for you, like when you tried to be the class clown in high school.

Your personality is a collection of traits that defines you as an individual and includes Anchors that you take pride in and Triggers that generate shame. You have a unique personality and a unique way of expressing yourself. There is "rightness" and "completeness" to the way you are. This "rightness" should not be confused with being "perfect" which is an unrealistic standard. When you believe that you are complete, whole, and right as you are, you recognize your value and worth. You recognize you are meant to be just as you are and that there is nothing missing or broken about you. You can take pride in your Anchors, but also understand that you need to be judicious in determining when you express them. You understand your Triggers and learn to work with them to modify their impact emotionally.

Arbitrary standards of perfection, which vary from culture to culture, can cause you to judge yourself based on specific characteristics such as traits and attributes, as well as physical beauty, sexual orientation, gender, race, nationality, religion, intelligence, or finances. These cultural norms and biases, however, deprive you of seeing the possibilities that only you have to offer. You cannot be anything you want to be. You need to work within the constraints of the possibilities that are available to you. For example, someone with little skill in Math is not apt to be successful in an accounting program of study. Or an individual who is rather humorless is not apt to become a successful stand-up comedian. Yet even within such constraints, the possibilities for your life are limited only by your imagination. There are many options, opportunities, and ideas just waiting for you to Dream Big!

> Richard wanted to be an athlete more than anything, however, his five foot three stature and slight build limited his opportunities in any major sport throughout elementary and middle school. He felt ashamed and disappointed that he could never attain what he truly desired. In high school he enjoyed sports vicariously by working at various jobs in the athletic department such as running the scoreboard and providing drinks for the team at breaks. Coach noticed that Richard was quick, decisive, and competent at executing any task that he gave Richard. Coach suggested that Richard enter the district training program for student referees. Richard jumped at the chance and performed well. He had found his niche, the place where he could use his talents in the environment that he loved.

Every thought, feeling, and action you express has importance and says something about you as a person. You have every trait and every trait has a place where it will be valued. Find the fit and you'll value every part of yourself. You become your best and most unique self when you put away your personal plan of improvement and take pride in being who you are. You set unrealistic goals by trying to look like or be like someone else, rather than by just trying to be more of yourself. You meet resistance and failure when you try to change who you are. For example, an exercise plan with a goal to firm and tone is bound to succeed, but an exercise plan with a goal of looking like a super model or a shapely actress is bound to fail. These efforts tap into your feelings of inadequacy and shame, your Triggers, and take you even farther away from being your best self. Often they lead you to give up completely, saying, "What's the use!?"

You will develop into the best you can be when you accept all parts of yourself. Follow your instincts, spend more time doing what you enjoy, and positive change will happen. Try getting caught up in the positive flow of your life. Resistance builds when you try to be someone you aren't. For example, in dieting, focusing on what you can't eat and what you shouldn't do builds resistance and causes you to feel defensive, which ultimately defeats you. When you try to follow a diet that doesn't tap into your interests and is too restrictive, you end up saying, "This diet won't work for me" and giving up entirely.

> Suzanne tried every popular diet that came along. She followed all the rules such as limiting calories or carbs, weighing and measuring her food, or eating a certain number of times a day. However, soon she would begin to break the rules because the foods on the diet were unappealing and the guidelines were too confining. She'd cheat with a brownie at book club, or a fast food purchase on her way to work. Eventually, Suzanne quit every diet and soon gained her excess weight back and more. Using arbitrary rules to control her diet created internal resistance. Suzanne needed to find an eating plan that worked best for her lifestyle. Reasonable guidelines might include: developing a list of healthy foods that she enjoyed eating, finding a fun way of adding exercise into her life, paying attention to her Body Talk, and learning to avoid using food as a reward. Developing her own unique path to better health and weight loss would be more likely to succeed.

Spend time enjoying who you are, your unique qualities and abilities, your distinctive traits and skills. Your combination of these is unmatched. There is no one else in the world quite like you, so enjoy being You.

You were born with a unique temperament and personality, but the environment, which includes parents, teachers, friends, co-workers, bosses, and society, shaped you and taught you to conform to circumstances — like being forced to be right-handed when you are left-handed. This molding of traits can be comfortable or uncomfortable depending on whether you felt accepted or not — whether you felt that the change was necessary or arbitrary to meet someone else's need for you to be a certain way.

As you mature, and value all parts of yourself, the parts you love and the parts you struggle with, you begin to live to your full potential — to be more of who you are. You have everything you need to be successful, happy, and loved. You have all traits within you and all are valuable and have a place. You don't need to get rid of parts of yourself; you need to understand and accept all of your parts. When you achieve self-acceptance, you become who you have always been, and you love yourself as you are and don't see the need to be anyone else. People often believe that change occurs by trying to get rid of various qualities within themselves; however, the opposite is actually true. Focus on who you are, be more of who you are, and recognize the value of a unique personality, and positive change will follow.

Charge Up Exercise Four
Use All of Your Traits!

Practice using all of your traits in the following ways:

1. List a few of the traits that you identified in the previous exercises as Anchors. In the second column "flip" the trait and write in the opposite trait, the Trigger. Finally, in the last column write about a situation where the "flipped" trait, the Trigger, actually worked for you. Notice how valuable your Triggers can be at the right time.

Trait (Anchor)	Flip the Trait (Trigger)	Situation Where the Flipped Trait Worked for You
Responsible	Irresponsible	I took a day off from work although it was a busy time.

2. List a few of the traits that you identified in the previous exercises as Anchors. In the second column write about a time when this Anchor became a liability and didn't work for you. Notice that Anchors can be overused.

Trait (Anchor)	Situation Where the Anchor Trait Didn't Work for You

3. List a few of the traits that you identified in the previous exercises as Triggers. In the second column write about a time when this Trigger actually worked for you.

Trait (Trigger)	Situation Where the Trigger Worked for You

Charge Up Your Life Milestones

A: Acceptance of the Whole

Now that you have finished A: Accept All Your Possibilities, what skills have you learned and what ones are you still working on?

- Put a check mark in front of the statements that feel true to you right now.
- Put a circle in front of the statements that you have not yet achieved.

____ I accept myself as I am.

____ I believe that as a whole person I have every trait in me to some degree.

____ I know that every trait I have is useful in one situation or another.

____ I notice when I am triggered by someone and recognize that it's more about me than them.

____ I believe that when I appreciate myself, good things happen.

____ My existence has a purpose in the world.

____ Procrastination is always intentional, and I pay attention to its message.

____ I acknowledge that when I'm working on being me, change takes place naturally.

_____ I notice what I'm not proud of, and I try to understand why.

_____ I avoid judging and limiting myself.

_____ I allow myself and others to be imperfect.

_____ I notice the traits in myself that I appreciate in others.

_____ The possibilities for my life are limited only by my imagination.

_____ I'm practicing using "A: Accept Your Possibilities" in the following ways:

_____

_____

_____

_____

_____

_____

_____

_____

_____

_____

_____

_____

A – Accept Your Possibilities

Additional Resources

The following is a list of suggested materials to help you on your journey to accessing all your possibilities:

* *All I Really Needed to Know I Learned in Kindergarten* by Robert Fulgrum – learn basic social behaviors found in our culture.

* *The Eagle's Secret: Success Strategies for Thriving at Work and in Life* by David McNally - strategies to help you gain personal achievement and success.

* *Temperament in Clinical Practice* by Stella Chess, and Alexander Thomas – explore how temperament is developed and expressed in your life.

* *The Four Agreements: A practical guide to personal freedom* by Don Miguel Ruiz – an inspiring book that reveals the source of self-limiting beliefs that create suffering and unhappiness.

* *Shame Lifter: Replacing Your Fears and Tears with Forgiveness, Truth, and Hope* by Marilyn Hontz – a spiritual guide to healing feelings of inadequacy and shame.

* *The Shadow Effect: Illuminating the hidden power of your true self* by Deepak Chopra, Debbie Ford, and Marianne Williamson – Three famous authors share their unique insights about the parts of ourselves we often deny yet drive our lives.

"…change occurs
when one becomes
what he is,
not when he tries to become
what he is not."

—*Arnold Beisser, 1970*
Paradoxical Theory of Change

R

Respectful Relationships

Conflict ←——→ Harmony

- Recognize Similarities
- Acknowledge Differences
- Interact with Diplomacy
- Establish Trust

"Build healthy interpersonal relations."

"What does this relationship
need from me,
not what do I need
from this relationship."

—Harville Hendrix
Clinical pastoral counselor
Author of Getting the Love You Want

$\mathcal{R}$: $\mathcal{R}$espec$\mathit{t}$ful $\mathcal{R}$ela$\mathit{t}$ionships

Conflict ◄─────► Harmony

$\mathcal{I}$n$\mathit{t}$ro$\mathit{d}$uc$\mathit{t}$ion

> Satisfying relationships can be brief or lasting. Cara, Naomi, Anastasia, and May had been friends since elementary school. As adult women with spouses and families they often remarked laughingly that in their 20-year friendship they had never argued and rarely even exchanged an angry word. Differences were quickly resolved and most of their time together was spent laughing and having fun. Not that they were alike: Cara was traditional and security oriented while Naomi was the free thinker who always seemed to be marching for a cause or supporting a movement somewhere. Anastasia was laid back and intellectual but May was opinionated and vocal. These young women found the keys to a satisfying relationship: common ground, tolerance for differences, respect, and trust.

Throughout your life, you form many relationships, with family, friends, and coworkers. They range from casual to intimate. Some connections are easy while others are more challenging. You might wonder why this is so. What are the ingredients of a good relationship and what's missing in those that are difficult? How do you create and maintain harmonious relationships? How do you improve a challenging relationship and, also, how can you make good relationships even better? These are some of the questions we'll be addressing in this chapter, R—Respectful Relationships, which discusses the four steps necessary to build healthy and effective interpersonal relationships: Recognize Similarities,

Acknowledge Differences, Interact with Diplomacy, and Establish Trust.

In this chapter you will read, first, that all people share basic needs and common goals: all people want to be happy and avoid pain. Next you'll consider that each person has a unique filter that is based on their temperament and experiences. It is used to interpret social situations, arrive at conclusions and make decisions. This filter explains why everyone doesn't look at situations in just the same way that you do. Also, you'll consider that how you speak to others, the words you use, as well as the tone in which you deliver them, communicates valuable information about how you feel and what you think. Finally, you'll see that trust is built when you do your part to set up a tolerant, safe environment for the relationship, one which avoids exploitation and fosters mutual benefit.

On the next page the Ambassador experience demonstrates the concept because ambassadors are masters of relationships. They are in the business of getting along with people from unfamiliar cultures and countries. They look for common ground, are sensitive to individual differences, speak diplomatically, and build trust. Ambassadors seek to achieve harmony, avoid conflict, and arrive at compromises that offer mutual benefit to all parties involved. You, too, can practice being an ambassador in your relationships, because individual people are a lot like foreign countries. Getting to know each one is challenging, but it can also be an exciting journey. As you begin to read, think of some relationships you'd like to understand better. Keep them in mind as you practice being an Ambassador in your contacts with others.

R
Ambassador Experience

Close your eyes and imagine yourself as an Ambassador whose prime goal is to communicate with others in a positive and productive manner. Breathe in the persona of one who acts in a thoughtful and diplomatic manner with everyone at home, at work, and in social situations. As an Ambassador, picture yourself looking for connections, things you have in common, with each of these people. Notice their unique personalities, how they differ from you in physical appearance, their interests, and their opinions. Consider what you could learn from each person, what you might ask them about themselves. Imagine listening to them without defensiveness, judgment or motive, just listening for understanding. Notice how open you are, and genuinely interested, in what the other person says, while you listen deeply for the underlying message. As an Ambassador, imagine being kind and thoughtful to those you encounter from day to day and seeing them as multifaceted and complex individuals.

What might that be like for you, to be an Ambassador who easily forms relationships and connections with others? Which of your traits would you need to call upon in order to acquire the diplomacy of the Ambassador?

What other traits or attributes might you need to develop in order to strengthen your relationships with others?

An Ambassador keeps in mind that every person is trying to get his own needs met. Acknowledging this allows an Ambassador to feel compassion for the other person and to step out of his personal perspective and into the other person's.

Practice being an Ambassador in your daily relationships.

R: Respectful Relationships

Step One: Recognize Similarities

Going to work, Frank often became frustrated with his fellow drivers. He saw them as "in his way" and as having less important goals than his own. After all, he needed to get to work! He honked his horn at drivers who got in front of him and shook his fist when someone made it difficult for him to switch lanes or moved slower than he thought they should. However, realistically, the other drivers were in the same position as he was. They were trying to get to work, too, and most likely felt frustrated about the traffic as well. The other drivers were more like Frank than not.

Every person in the world is more like you than not because human beings have a shared reality. We all have the capacity to feel happiness, sadness, anger, and fear and we all desire to experience pleasure and avoid pain. As human beings, we have a common desire to be understood, respected, and cared for.

In order to truly relate to another person you must discover a human connection, by looking for similarities—common interests, shared traits, and mutual experiences. Some examples of basic similarities are: gender, marital status, children, extended family, sports interests, hobbies, style of dress, age, or favorite foods. Also, consider any of the traits you might share, such as analytical skills, sense of humor, curiosity about new technology, or any of the traits in the Trait Box in A: **Accept Your Possibilities**. It's easier to find similarities with people you relate to well, but the challenge is to discover those same human traits and qualities in those individuals with whom you have difficulty relating.

It is, however, most important to look for and acknowledge common humanness, such as a need for safety, food, shelter, love, respect, and acceptance. Everyone looks for opportunities to bring love, happiness, and success into his or her life. For example, Jeff brings love into his life by socializing with his friends while April brings success into her life by closely monitoring her brokerage account. Jeff and April might not be meeting their needs in the same way that you do, but they have the same underlying reasons. Now think about the common human traits you share with the people in your life and the ways in which you each express them. In what ways do others bring love, happiness, and success into their lives through their basic human needs? These needs form a human connection among us all and are the simplest elements of any relationship. When you notice common humanness, you are essentially saying, "I recognize that we are one."

When you see others as being like you, you treat them as you would like to be treated, because you understand that you both want the same things. This is often referred to as the Golden Rule and some variation of it can be found in all religions and spiritual philosophies. This rule instructs you to step away from your own filtered viewpoint and to try to see things from the perspective of the other person, like Satinder does in the story which follows:

> Satinder was a regular at all of her friends' parties because just having her there seemed to create a fun and relaxing atmosphere. No one was left sitting alone because she knew how to get even the shyest person talking or involved in games. Everyone who was at a party with Satinder seemed to have a good time. When asked about how she did this, she laughed and said she just imagined how it would be if she was the other person. They all want to be happy and have a good time. She knew what it was like not knowing how to fit in at times. She treated them as she would like to be treated in a similar situation. Little wonder Satinder worked in sales and marketing where her ability to read people and create bonds worked like magic.

When you see this common humanness in others, you act and speak in ways that communicate "You're just like me." In the first chapter, C: Compliment and Nurture, you saw that self-involvement is acceptable and expected in babies. They feel that their world revolves totally around them and they are oblivious to the common human needs of others. But as they grow they start to see that others have wants and needs too, just like them. Have you ever seen the look of surprise on a toddler's face when someone hits them back or takes the toy that they just took from someone else? They're starting to see that others have the same needs that they do. When they learn to ask and not grab, to talk and not hit, to share and not hoard, they're not only demonstrating good social skills, they're noticing common humanness. All the other kids have the same needs and wants as they do. Adults who remain in the self-involved phase of childhood, viewing things only from their own perspective, have difficulty developing healthy, interpersonal relationships. They are failing to notice common human needs.

This understanding of common needs and wants evolves into conscience, when it is combined with a sense of right and wrong. Your conscience directs you to pause and consider the perspective of the other person before acting. This is a step beyond the Golden Rule because you treat people well, not only by seeing their common human needs, but because it's the right thing to do. You empathize and feel compassion for others because you can share someone else's feelings. It isn't necessary to have identical experiences, such as losing your job, being diagnosed with cancer, or having your daughter win a lucrative scholarship, in order to understand what loss, disappointment, and pride feel like. You understand because you've experienced those feelings, in other situations. The underlying feeling establishes the common human link, not the event in which it occurred.

> Eugene, a police officer, was called upon to apprehend a transient. The man was dirty, unkempt, and noncompliant. Eugene resisted the urge to view this individual as less than himself by treating him in a condescending or authoritative manner. Instead, Eugene recognized the transient as a fellow human being who was caught in challenging circumstances. He recognized the man's underlying feelings of shame and anger at being in this situation. As a result he reacted with empathy and compassion and treated the man with dignity and respect. Eugene was able to connect with the humanity of the man's pain and suffering, and do the right thing.

Understanding this human connection fosters empathy and compassion. As fellow human beings we understand one another's disappointment, joy, and sadness because these underlying emotions permeate our lives as humans. When you show compassion for others, you take their perspective and understand their point of view by knowing that their basic feelings are similar to yours.

The hallmark of seeing others as being like you is to treat others in an I-Thou manner, (see Buber on resource page). This happens when you see the worth of the other person. You notice that they have value and significance in the world just by being alive, regardless of how much money they have, where they work, or what they own. In an I-Thou relationship, people see one another as equal in their humanness and treat one another with the respect and dignity that they deserve.

When you relate in an I-Thou manner, you say "I see you. You are worthy of my attention and respect." When You relate in this manner, in brief encounters or in lasting relationships, you treat people well because you see their basic importance. Both people are saying, "I see you as worthy. I recognize that you see me that way too." I-Thou relationships are horizontal in structure and are based on recognition of the common worth and value of the participants. They forge bonds because they communicate respect.

The opposite of an I-Thou relationship is an I-It relationship, in which one person sees the other person in parts and judges him or her as less than, by focusing on isolated qualities, such as gender, financial worth, job or ethnicity. In an I-It relationship you say, "I don't see you as a multi-dimensional human being, just like me. To me, you don't matter."

For example, the woman who walks through the checkout line at the grocery store chatting on her cell phone and barely acknowledging the checker with either eye contact or words is having an I-It relationship with the checker. He is barely worth her notice. He is the "checker" and not, in her awareness, a human being who is just as important as she is. Or have you ever been on a date when the other person talks all about themselves and never asks you anything? Did you feel dehumanized, like you weren't important and had nothing to contribute. I-It relationships, which are vertical in structure, focus on differences and create separation and detachment.

Elizabeth remembered being pregnant with her 3rd child in the early 70's, the days of feminism. During shopping excursions, she struggled to manage two toddlers, push a cart, and open doors. She was often surprised to have young women of her age slam doors in her face and give her angry looks. One actually stated, "Haven't you heard of the pill?" These women saw Elizabeth one-dimensionally, as someone who did not share their values on family planning. They failed to see her other qualities: she was a caring, educated young woman who chose to have her family young and forego her career for a few years. She was more like them than not; she deserved their respect.

A man is having an I-It relationship with a woman when he focuses on her body parts and not her worth as a human being. A woman who sees a man in terms of his bank account is also seeing him one-dimensionally. I-It relationships are judgmental and divisive, while I-Thou relationships are open and inclusive.

Charge Up Exercise One
Recognize Similarities!

1. List a few individuals with whom you have good relationships. List the identifiers and interests you share. Some examples are gender, marital status, children, extended family, sports interests, hobbies, style of dress, age, or favorite foods. Also, consider any of the traits you share, such as laughing at the same types of jokes, both liking to be right, or any of the traits in the Trait Box in A: Accept Your Possibilities.

	Names: Good Relationships	**Common Human Traits**
1		
2		
3		
4		

2. Now list the names of a few people with whom you have conflict, perhaps a coworker, relative, or an acquaintance. Imagine having an I-Thou relationship where you share common needs, wants, and goals. It's easier to find similarities with people you relate to well, but challenge yourself to discover those same human traits and qualities in those individuals who are difficult for you to relate to.

	Names: Difficult Relationships	Common Human Traits
1		
2		
3		
4		

When you see the commonalities that human beings share, you see people as being equal to you and as having as much value in the world as you do. You see people in a "horizontal" way, and you have an I-Thou relationship. When you view others as being less or more than you or as having a hierarchical value in the world, you rank people in importance "vertically," and you have an I-It relationship.

R: Respectful Relationships
Step Two: Acknowledge Differences

As a young child, Stan was even-tempered, patient, and flexible. He socialized well and rarely fussed or complained. However, as he grew older, his high–achieving parents worried that he wasn't more assertive and competitive. After all, those were the traits that got them where they were and how could Stan be a success in life otherwise? But Stan was never the star on the soccer team, or the president of his class, or an honors student. In reality, Stan was happy being who he was, despite his parents' well-meaning wishes for him. He enjoyed his friends, did reasonably well in school, and was happy being one of the team rather than the star. As an adult, Stan's flexible and tolerant nature was valuable in his position as accounts manager for an internet start-up company. He was able to work collaboratively and he adapted easily to the ever-changing business environment. Stan proved to be quite successful being just who he was, rather than by trying to become someone he wasn't.

Although you have much in common with every other human being, you are still unique. Everything you think, feel, and do is interpreted by your personal filter, which is different from anyone else's filter. No one can know you as well as you know yourself. No one can understand you until they learn about the unique way in which you view the world.

Your personal filter is a combination of temperamental characteristics and life experiences. Your temperament, first discussed in Chapter A, is inborn and largely out of your control. You can modify your temperamental traits but you won't be successful at changing them entirely. Adaptability to change; distractibility; persistence; intensity of reactions; tolerance for frustration; quality of mood; and ease of sociability are some general categories of temperament. How would you rate your temperamental characteristics? Your life experiences are shaped by your race, age, class, genetics, sexual preferences, culture, and family background. From both your temperament and experiences, you develop a filter that you use to make decisions, form opinions, and modify attitudes. These elements combine to form a very unique individual, you. You bring this unique filter to every encounter you have. Everyone you meet brings their personal filter to the encounter as well.

The challenge in relationships is to make room for and value everyone just as they are. To develop new relationships and enhance the ones you already have, notice the unique personality and perspective of the other person. What do you see? If you watch closely, every person communicates valuable information to you about them. Their words and actions tell you about their temperament, experiences, opinions, attitudes, and judgments.

Making room for differences is an important ingredient in healthy relationships that starts at the level of the family. We are often surprised when siblings raised in the same home emerge as distinct individuals - some are like their parents and others are different. This is because each child is unique, and healthy parenting involves nurturing the children's differences as well as their similarities.

> Maria and Patrick were introverts, but their children were definite extroverts. It was often difficult for the couple to understand their children's need for social contact, and the children found their parents' need for solitude to be puzzling as well. So, to recognize these differences, Maria and Patrick provided activities for the children to participate in with peers and moved a bit out of their cocoon of solitude. The children, in turn, learned to give Mom and Dad some space within the home for quiet time. Understanding and valuing their different perspectives was a challenge for the entire family, but necessary for the growth of each individual. Each family member recognized that the other members, although quite different in some ways, were okay as they were. The differences didn't need to communicate dissent. The differences communicated the richness and variability found in this family's dynamics. So, too, it is in society.

What you learned about making room for differences in your family extends out into society in your relationships with friends, coworkers, and intimate partners. Relationships are enriched when you are curious about differences and make room for them; however, relationships are damaged when you see your viewpoint as the only way to interpret the world. You must modify your ego-centric perspective in order to truly communicate with others. You understand different perspectives by showing interest in what others think and feel.

Can you recall a time when you met someone new: maybe new neighbors or a new coworker in your department? Questions probably came up in your mind because you're curious about these new people. If you're going to be living next door to someone, you want to get to know them and find out about their interests and their lifestyle. If you're going to be working closely with someone, you want to know about their work habits, quirks, and skills. Your curiosity is piqued, so you ask questions. When you want to have a relationship with someone, you reach out to discover more about them.

When you consider all the differences there are in the world, in experiences and temperament, and how these elements are combined in billions of ways to create individual people, you begin to see the wealth of variability that the world has to offer. People are definitely more alike than not, but each one is unique.

To understand how differences merge but can also retain their individuality, consider the place on the beach where the sand and the ocean meet as their point of contact. The sand and ocean can meet and blend but each element retains its own essence. You will never confuse sand with water, yet you can see them together in your hand when you scoop up a handful of both. If the sand and the ocean weren't different, there could be no contact between them. If the sand and the ocean were alike, they would simply blend and have no discernible boundaries, like when you mix up the ingredients for cookies in a bowl. You can no longer tell where the flour ends and the water, oil, and eggs begin because they have merged and formed a new and different whole. This blending and merging at the point of contact also happens in relationships. Communication begins at the point where similarities are acknowledged and deepens when differences are recognized. So, when you and a friend have a discussion on which candidate to vote for, your points of difference form the basis of the dialogue. If you both felt the same way about each candidate then you'd probably just echo each other's opinions. There would be no differences in thought on the subject so there would be no points of contact to explore.

As another example, have you ever noticed a long-married couple out for dinner together who say little to each other except sparsely interjected brief comments? Perhaps they have lost the edges, the points of contact that caused them to talk for hours at a time when they first met. Depending on who the people are, this can be a comfortable place to be, one that has been achieved after many years. Or, the relationship can be a wasteland of communication, one that has lost its allure and luster and is no longer intriguing and exciting. If so, interjecting some differences, some points of contact, can revive a deteriorating relationship. If the couple makes some new friends, or engages in a new hobby or interest together or separately and shares it, the relationship will have new life.

The more that you recognize and appreciate differences, the more you are able to forge new relationships. By combining recognition of human commonalities with recognition of others' unique perspectives, you can see other individuals as whole people. Knowing how you are alike and how you are different are both necessary for making contact and developing a relationship.

Differences, however, can create conflict if you feel threatened or criticized. For instance, if you like classical music and someone in your group openly criticizes it as outdated and pretentious, you have a choice to make. You can consider this is just this person's opinion and decide to either open a discussion on the merits of classical music or remain silent and just listen, looking for more understanding of the viewpoint. You can also, instead, feel personally criticized by this person's negativity about something you enjoy, and fight back defensively asserting your own viewpoint, and criticizing theirs. Differences can invite curiosity or promote anger; it's entirely the choice of the individuals involved.

One possible explanation, for defensive reactions to differences, is that humans have been programmed from their earliest stages of development, in prehistoric times, to assess whether or not they were safe. If not, they needed to move into a defensive posture "to fight or flee" to protect themselves. Those primal instincts are very helpful at times such as when you're walking alone down a dimly lit street and you sense someone behind you. You feel fear and honor your instincts by fleeing, which is appropriate.

It's important, however, to be aware that this same instinctual fear of others can be misplaced and directed toward those who present no real danger. Your fears can be targeted at those who differ from you in ethnicity, race, religion, sexuality, and sometimes towards others who just hold an opposing opinion. These differences can generate fear, create distance, and result in a defensive reaction where conflict and animosity waste energy.

The best way to discern whether a situation is dangerous or harmless is to pay attention and stay present with what is truly occurring. Check out your internal warning signs and cognitively assess the situation. Decide whether this is truly a fight-or-flight situation. As in our earlier example about music, do you really need to have everyone agree with your tastes? Can you be an individual and just honor your own preferences, without feeling angry with those who disagree?

Charge Up Exercise Two
Acknowledge Differences!

Practice noticing the uniqueness of others by trying out the following:

1. While speaking with others, notice their unique qualities, such as the melody of their voice, the tempo of their speech, or the particular way they say their words. Spend time noticing the other person's physical appearance, their manner of dress and their needs and motivations. What makes him or her unique? What do you notice?

_____

_____

_____

_____

2. Seek out one or more individuals with whom you normally would not interact. Be curious and inquisitive and discover what can be learned by getting to know someone new and different from you. Whom did you choose? What did you notice?

_____

_____

_____

_____

3. Choose an individual you find particularly challenging. What are the traits that cause conflict with you? How does each relate to the unique experiences that person may have had? How can you show an appreciation for these differences? Remember, appreciation does not necessarily indicate agreement. You can appreciate individuality without changing who you are. Write your thoughts below.

_____

_____

_____

_____

4. Think of a few close friends. How are you different? How do you show appreciation for these differences? How do you avoid conflict over them?

_____

_____

_____

_____

Step Three: Interact with Diplomacy

Celia was frustrated with her partner, Rosemary, who sometimes just didn't listen. They were decorating their new apartment and Celia had lots of ideas for colors and placement of furniture. She wanted to talk about her ideas and get Rosemary's opinion on each one, but Rosemary was a problem solver not a talker. She just wanted to make a decision and move on. This trait worked well when they needed a simple solution to a problem, but was annoying when Celia wanted to discuss an issue. So when Celia brought up the topic of a color for their new sofa, Rosemary's quick response was "Red, I like red" and that was the end of the discussion. Celia felt unheard and dissatisfied with their otherwise good relationship. Rosemary didn't acknowledge Celia's interest in making their home beautiful and comfortable. She didn't question Celia about her ideas and her preferences. Couldn't Rosemary see how frustrated Celia was? Rosemary needed to move out of her comfort zone and learn to make better contact with Celia.

Have you ever been in a conversation with a coworker, friend, or family member and walked away or hung up the phone upset and frustrated because you didn't feel heard? Have you found yourself resorting to name-calling or gossip because of your aggravation with this person, "who never stops talking" or who "never asks your opinion"? If so, you can relate to the frustration of not being able to communicate your views and feelings, because you don't feel heard.

Diplomacy, the protocols and language that ambassadors use in respectful communication, is missing in interactions like these. Diplomacy involves making physical, mental, and emotional contact with the person you are speaking to. Without contact between listener and speaker, no communication is really taking place.

When you make physical contact, you use your body to communicate by smiling, nodding, and making eye contact. You let the speaker know that you are paying attention. With individuals that you know well, a touch on the arm or hand establishes more personal contact. When you aren't communicating with your body, speakers feel that they are not being heard.

Matthew was an adept multi-tasker; he was able to type, listen, and carry on a conversation simultaneously. He was also, as you might have guessed, a high-energy worker who seldom took breaks. When a coworker approached him, he often continued on with what he was doing while he responded. He felt good about being able to do more than one thing at once and, as a result, he accomplished a great deal of work. His coworkers, however, felt slighted and dismissed by what they felt was disrespectful behavior. When a friend pointed out how his behavior was interpreted by his coworkers, Matthew understood their position, although he had never thought of it that way before. Subsequently, when he was approached by a coworker, he made an effort to stop what he was doing, or let his coworker know he needed a minute to finish what he was doing, before he responded. Matthew was learning to demonstrate physical contact in communication.

Next, mental contact involves communicating effectively on a cognitive level by choosing your words, taking ownership of your thoughts and opinions, checking out assumptions, and asking clarifying questions.

First, choose words to communicate your thoughts that will be understood by your audience. For example, when speaking to a child, you wouldn't use complex vocabulary; similarly, a professional would not use jargon when speaking to a group of non-professionals. When you are cognizant of what words your listener understands, you are demonstrating an I-Thou relationship, as discussed in Recognize Similarities. You are setting up communication on a "level playing field" and not trying to one-up your listener by flaunting unfamiliar vocabulary or using complex examples to make a point.

Next, "I" statements communicate ownership of your ideas. Sometimes you may notice individuals using the collective "you"; for example, when they say "You always feel bad when you're in conflict with a friend" instead of taking full ownership of the statement by saying, "I always feel bad when I am in conflict with a friend." See the difference? Notice when you distance yourself from owning your words by using "you" instead of "I." Also, "you" can be used in an accusatory manner and is likely to make the listener defensive. For example, consider the simple difference between, "You never listen to me," and "I feel you don't listen to me." The first sentence is accusatory and makes a statement like it is an absolute fact, but the second one is offering an opinion and the speaker is taking ownership of the statement.

Also, a good mental communicator "checks out" assumptions before drawing conclusions about what someone else might have meant. Each of us interprets our world through our personal filter; this tendency to see the world our way requires us to check out assumptions to determine if what we heard was actually what the other person meant to say. If you hear something that causes you to feel defensive, angry, or insulted, check it out! Say something like, "When you said_____, I felt_____. Were you intending that?" or "Can you say that in another way? The words you used made me feel_____?" If the person you are communicating with truly wants to relate to you respectfully, he will listen to your request and try using more neutral language.

To explore the use of language in communication, try discussing an issue or an event with a friend or loved one using this simple technique: First, speaker #1 gives an opinion or summary of the issue. Then, speaker #2 tries to restate what speaker #1 just said (e.g., "I heard you say ..."). Next, speaker #1 clarifies the points that speaker #2 did not get quite right (e.g., "That's not quite right. I said...") and so on until both speaker and listener are sending and receiving the same message. Now switch places and have speaker #2 give an opinion or summary of the issue and have speaker #1 restate it, and so on. You'll find that both individuals' personal filters get in the way of their listening.

Have you ever played the "telephone game"? Several people sit in a row and the 1ˢᵗ person whispers a statement to the second person and so on down the line to the end, when the final person repeats what she has just been told. Rarely does the last statement match the initial statement because our personal filters change, even subtly, what we have heard.

Finally, mental contact in communication involves being curious about what the other person is saying, why they're saying it, and where their opinions are coming from. In daily communication, if you feel confused, puzzled, or unsure of what you're hearing, ask questions. Once again, be sure that you received the actual message that the speaker sent. When you truly pay attention and listen to the speaker, you aren't simply biding your time and waiting for your turn to speak. You are interested in what the speaker says, and you want the speaker to know this. When the speaker finishes, ask a question or make a comment or gesture to show that you were really listening.

For example, if a friend tells you about his child's latest accomplishment, acknowledge that you have heard the speaker and don't immediately launch into a similar story about your child. After all, this story belongs to your friend and is not simply a prompt for you to share something about your life. Notice how often individuals "trade stories," without ever really listening to one another and showing an interest in what they've heard. Or, a wife will talk about her day and her husband will respond with a story about his day rather than drawing out her story with questions that indicate interest. At times, it can be fun to have your spouse tell a similar story that communicates shared interests and common feelings, but at other times it can feel discounting, like your spouse doesn't really listen to you. It can seem like you're just talking to yourself while your spouse or partner is just waiting to speak again. Try a new way to communicate and see if your spouse notices you're using a new method. Staying present with the speaker and listening intently takes your communication to a higher level.

The third type of contact in communication is emotional contact, which involves understanding the feelings and emotional perspective of the speaker and avoiding giving unsolicited advice.

On a trip to southeast Asia, Tara spoke to a Cambodian shopkeeper. Regardless of what Tara said to him about the scarves she was considering purchasing, the shopkeeper nodded, smiled and acknowledged her point: Yes, there was a slight flaw in the material, yes, the color was not a deep blue, and yes, perhaps she could find the item for a cheaper price somewhere else. The shopkeeper did not disagree about anything and maintained a friendly, pleasant demeanor. Tara, as a result, did not have the opportunity to become defensive, which could have occurred if the shopkeeper disagreed with her and defended his products. This congenial, emotional contact established "flow." Both the buyer and the seller were in agreement; they were "on the same page" which increased Tara's willingness to purchase several scarves. Their interaction may have been influenced by a language barrier to some degree, and smiling and agreeing might have been the way the shopkeeper functioned, but it's also likely that this successful shopkeeper understood how to make emotional contact with his customers.

A good communicator avoids giving unsolicited advice. Consider that when you give advice, you are subtly communicating that the listener isn't capable of solving her problem by herself. Your kind and thoughtful gesture actually communicates that the listener can't find a way out of her current issue. Instead, try asking clarifying questions that assist the listener in thinking through her dilemma, such as "tell me more about that," or "what was that experience like for you?" Also, many times a problem to one person is not a problem to another. Sometimes you might just want someone to listen to your problem and offer some solicitous comments or show interest through some thoughtful questions. Getting unsolicited advice, then, can make you feel bad and become defensive. A good listener develops a positive emotional bond with a speaker, like using the AAA Method in the following example.

Austin's teenage son, Terry, was upset that he had received a poor grade on a recent Social Studies test. He felt his teacher had graded him too harshly on his essay responses. Austin's first instinct was to try to fix the problem and offer some suggestions, but he decided to try the AAA Method. Austin first Acknowledged that Terry was upset and stated that he could see how disappointed Terry was in his grade. He recalled that he had seen Terry studying over the past few days. Terry looked over at his dad, visibly calmed down and said, "Yes, I worked so hard." Then, Austin Asked Questions. He inquired about the test and what Terry thought about it and what he might have heard other students say. To Austin's surprise, Terry kept talking about the test; he admitted that some students found the test hard and the grading of the questions harsh, yet others did well on it. Terry was confused about the teacher's method of grading. Austin had Terry's attention and so he took a chance and offered some Advice. Austin's advice to his son was to *request some one-on-one time with the teacher to get clarification on what the teacher had been looking for in the responses. Terry, once again to his dad's surprise, said he would consider it. The AAA Method worked in this situation because Terry felt heard when his dad first made emotional contact with him. Austin didn't immediately launch into giving advice because it would have subtly communicated to Terry that his dad had all the answers and Terry wasn't capable of handling the situation. Using the AAA Method established emotional contact that led to real communication. Because Terry felt heard by his dad, in turn, he was willing to hear his dad's advice.*

The AAA Method is an excellent way of communicating respectfully that works with spouses, friends, and coworkers who are voicing a problem. Try the AAA Method: Acknowledge the emotion, Ask Questions, and give Advice, "in that order," and watch your relationships grow. Often you will find that working through the first two A's is enough and you don't need to use the 3rd. Problems have a way of working themselves out when people feel acknowledged and are given the opportunity to independently express their thoughts on a subject as well as their ideas for a solution.

In summary, diplomacy involves an awareness of people's similarities and differences— as well as physical, cognitive, and emotional contact with them. All of these help build deep and enduring relationships because they show respectful intentions and a willingness to forge bonds that are mutually beneficial.

Charge Up Exercise Three
Interact with Diplomacy!

Practice speaking diplomatically in your conversations with others by doing the following:

1. The next time a friend, relative, or colleague comes to you with a problem try listening for the underlying feelings instead of trying to solve the problem by giving advice. Instead of getting involved in the content of the story, ask open-ended questions until you determine whether the person is happy, sad, angry, or scared, or some variation of these. What did you discover?

_____

_____

_____

2. Next, acknowledge the speaker's feelings with words such as "It sounds like you felt very sad." Ask more questions to draw out the story, for example, "What was that like for you?" Avoid giving unsolicited advice. See how comfortable it is for you to simply notice the feeling and ask questions, without offering your own advice. Write about your experience.

_____

_____

_____

R: Respectful Relationships

Step Four: Establish Trust

Bernadette and Charlene were co-owners of an art gallery. Bernadette was the more business minded partner and she watched the bottom line: setting prices, negotiating rents, and buying advertising. Charlene was the people person who finessed the customers, set up the shows, and communicated on a personal level with the artists. Each partner recognized that the success of their business was a joint effort and that neither partner was ultimately more valuable. Over the years of their prosperous enterprise they had learned to stop keeping score about who was working harder. Each trusted the other to work in the best interests of their business.

Relationships that are deep, long-lasting, and beneficial have trust at their foundation. To achieve trust, you must treat the other person as you would want to be treated, acknowledge your similarities, accept your differences, and speak diplomatically. Trust is firmly established when you avoid mind reading, allow the relationship to proceed without judgment, communicate reciprocity and mutual benefit, and avoid keeping score. By following these tips, you can establish meaningful and long-lasting relationships.

When you decide whether to speak your truth, you ask yourself, "Will this person accept me as I am?" and "Can I trust this person if I make my authentic self visible?" For instance, if your boss only wants to hear good news and doesn't like hearing about problems, how authentic can your interactions be? Also, if your spouse is apt to be critical when you express your dissatisfaction with your job, how much do you feel like sharing? You censor your words and filter what you hear based on how much you trust the other person.

The first step to positive communication is to believe that each person speaks sincerely and honestly. If you want to share ideas and work together, it is important that you trust and believe that each person speaks sincerely and honestly. When you adopt a suspicious attitude and engage in "mind reading" of others by making statements such as, "You don't really feel that way" or "You're really mad" rather than taking the person's behavior and statements at face value, discord results. Recall from the previous section, "Interact With Diplomacy" that "you" statements such as these invite defensiveness because they subtly accuse the other person of dishonesty. It makes the person feel like a liar, that he is untrustworthy and unsafe in your company. Can you think of a quicker way to destroy a relationship than to call a person a liar?

Lucinda and David are a young couple whose disagreements quickly turn into shouting matches over the simplest of issues due to their tendency to use "you" statements and mind read. During a recent discussion of which restaurant to choose for dinner, Lucinda suggested Mylee's for Chinese. David responded, "You don't like that place, why would you suggest it?" Lucinda retorted that she did like it but from time to time wasn't in the mood for Chinese, and David continued the repartee by saying that she never liked it and that he wasn't going to listen to her complaining. Then Lucinda accused David of always having to be right and telling her what she was thinking and on and on. Do you get the idea? If David had simply noted that the last time they were there Lucinda didn't like her meal and took her response at face value, the issue would never have escalated. They could have chosen the restaurant or selected another.

Intimate partners often feel they know one another well enough to read his or her mind but doing this can slowly erode trust in these very important relationships. Partners often feel the need to be completely validated by the other at all times, so they insist on having common thoughts and common impressions. And so the partners need to rehash and dissect any disagreement until they reach perfect agreement or perfect chaos. They resist seeing that the other person is "and will always be" a separate person who won't ever be figured out entirely. One day you might like something and the next day you don't. What's wrong with that? Disagreements erode the bonds of intimacy and make the partner being accused feel unworthy. Who can feel safe when they don't feel worthy? In the case of Lucinda and David, both partners needed to be validated and accepted, but instead both felt shame from the other's accusations and mind reading. Think back to our discussion of guilt and shame in the Understand Your Triggers section in A: Accept Your Possibilities. When you have done something wrong, you feel guilty, but when you feel wrong, such as when you are accused of being dishonest, you feel shame. You want to stay away from rather than be with someone who shames you.

Instead of mind reading, try trusting the person who says she feels a certain way or who maintains that he is not angry even if you think he looks otherwise. Sometimes people aren't ready to disclose information, or they don't have the coping skills to be more open. Have you ever had someone observe that you "look angry" when you simply weren't ready to discuss a situation, when you just wanted to pretend it hadn't happened until you were ready to discuss it? Feeling pressured to be ready for something when you aren't just increases your discomfort. When you display trust and have compassion for where the other person is at that point in time, you are able to step away from, rather than toward a conflict. You can only speak your own truth, and you can't force others to be ready to do the same. By establishing a kind and tolerant environment so others can speak their truths, when they are ready, you open the door for respectful communication to occur.

Another way to build trust is to adopt the social perspective of the other person, by considering that there can be opinions other than yours that, in the eyes of the other person, have great validity. Black-and-white thinking is the view that there is one right answer and that all other options are wrong. This leads to divisiveness and invites conflict because, to be right, everyone must agree with you. Instead, consider that there are very few opinions that are absolutely right and that most opinions fall in the gray area, where the perspective of the person determines the "rightness" of the opinion. It is not always necessary to judge someone else's opinion as right or wrong, or to debate its merits. Sometimes it is enough to simply accept it as the opinion of another person and stop there. Simple remarks such as "I see where you're coming from" or "I understand your point of view" communicate acceptance but not necessarily agreement. You set up a congenial and trusting environment when you make it safe for others to express differing opinions and reduce the anxiety that results when people need to consider how their words will be received.

Trust also involves the expectation of reciprocity, whether immediate or delayed. In relationships, you may often expect to be repaid for each kindness you extend and be acknowledged for each concession you offer, but, realistically, this does not occur and may not be possible. A respectful communicator puts away the imaginary score card and simply allows the relationship to continue. There will be times when the other person repays you for your kindnesses and others when he or she does not. Overall, the ledger is usually pretty equal but you aren't always aware of that fact. Often you may not know when someone else has put in a kind word for you or otherwise helped you out. Allow yourself to trust that forces in the universe work for your benefit, and work diligently to offer kindness and fair treatment to you and others; avoid focusing on whether you will be repaid, which generates ill will and takes you out of your present experience.

Finally, trust involves the expectation of mutual benefit. For example, "I trust that my friend is saying his words with my interests in mind and does not intend to victimize or manipulate me in any way." It's easier to believe a good friend than it is to believe someone who you do not know as well.

> Carson, Arthur, and Adam worked together in a competitive office environment. Carson had been working overtime to complete several bids, and his best friend Arthur suggested he take the evening off and start up again the next day more refreshed. Arthur noticed that his friend Carson looked tired, and he suggested going for a drink to relax. Adam also noticed Carson's heavy workload and remarked that Carson should take a break because the work always gets done, right? How Carson took both of these suggestions differed dramatically. Carson listened to Arthur because he felt no mistrust, but he sensed manipulation from Adam, one of his competitors. He believed Adam would like to see him fall behind so he could jump ahead. Both coworkers were giving the same advice, but Carson interpreted each coworker differently. It's the same in our relationships that have trust at their core.

Some exercises follow that will help you to practice the four steps of respectful communication. Incorporate them into your daily interactions and watch your relationships with family, coworkers, and friends deepen and grow.

Charge Up Exercise Four
Establish Trust!

Explore your trust levels with others by doing the following:

1. Below, list the people in your life whom you truly trust. Next to each name, jot down what you believe makes them trustworthy.

People I Trust	What makes them trustworthy?

2. Next, list the people in your life whom you do not trust or whose trust you have lost and explain why.

People I Don't Trust	What makes them untrustworthy?

3. How do you build trust in a relationship? What do you do to make others feel emotionally safe? How could you communicate that you are trustworthy more effectively in your relationships? Write your thoughts below.

_____

_____

_____

_____

_____

_____

_____

4. In what ways do you inspire trust in others? In what ways can others count on you to make them feel emotionally safe? Which of your behaviors might cause others to mistrust you? In what ways can others distrust you? Explore these areas of trust and see what comes up for you.

_____

_____

_____

_____

_____

_____

_____

Charge Up Your Life Milestones

R: Respectful Relationships

Now that you have finished R: Respectful Relationships, what skills have you learned and what ones are you still working on?

- Put a check mark in front of the statements that feel true to you right now.
- Mark a circle in front of the statements that you have not yet achieved.

_____ I take ownership of my words by using "I" statements.

_____ I avoid "you" statements because they make others defensive.

_____ I am curious and interested in others' ideas and opinions.

_____ I take responsibility for my own thoughts and feelings.

_____ I treat others in the way I want to be treated by communicating respectfully.

_____ I ask questions more than I give advice.

_____ I can acknowledge another person's opinion without having to agree.

_____ I avoid mind-reading and I check out my assumptions.

_____ When I notice I am being defensive, I am curious about why.

_____ I provide a kind and tolerant environment for honest dialogue.

_____ I acknowledge that everything I think and feel doesn't need to be said.

_____ I notice and value the rich uniqueness and differences in others.

_____ I see others as equals and view them horizontally rather than vertically.

_____ I am practicing using "R: Respectful Relationships," in the following ways:

_____

_____

_____

_____

_____

_____

_____

_____

_____

_____

_____

_____

_____

_____

_____

_____

_____

R – Respectful Relationships

Additional Resources

The following is a list of suggested materials to help you on your journey to forming respectful relationships:

* *Nonviolent Communication: A Language of Life*, 2nd Edition by Marshall B. Rosenberg, Ph.D. – understand social structures and how to develop relationships based on respect, compassion, and cooperation.

* *Getting the Love You Want: A Guide for Couples* by Harville Hendrix, Ph.D. – An in depth understanding of the psychology of love and relationships.

* *I and Thou* by Martin Buber, Walter Kaufman (translator), and S.G. Smith (translator) – the classic guide to human interactions, which can be either vertical or horizontal.

* *You're Wearing That?: Understanding Mothers and Daughters in Conversation* by Deborah Tannen – an insightful look at this complex relationship, the elements of which can easily be applied to others.

* *If the Buddha Married: Creating Enduring Relationships on a Spiritual Path* by Charlotte Kasl – a whimsical look at respectful relating within intimate relationships.

* *Whale Done!: The Power of Positive Relationships* by Kenneth H. Blanchard, Jim Ballard, Chuck Thompkins, and Thad Lacinak – an easy-to-read look at the benefits of focusing on the positive in relationships.

"The real art of conversation
is not only to say the right thing in the right
place but to leave unsaid the wrong thing
at the tempting moment."

—Dorothy Nevill
English Writer

Genuine and Authentic

Unhealthy Boundaries ◄──────► Integrity

- Know What You Stand For
- Live in Your Circle of Integrity
- Handle External Pressures
- Make Ethical Choices

"Know who you are and own it."

"Happiness is when
what you think,
what you say,
and what you do
are in harmony."

—Mohandas Gandhi
Spiritual leader of India
Advocate for non-violence
(1869–1948)

G: Genuine and Authentic
Unhealthy Boundaries ←——→ Integrity

Introduction

> Becky had a strong need to get along with others. She was accommodating, pleasant, and generally a peacemaker at work and with friends. Problems occurred, however, when friends or coworkers were divided on an issue and they each looked to Becky for support. Becky worried so much about disappointing someone that she was afraid to offer her opinion. Sometimes she felt like she didn't even know what her opinion actually was because her need to please was so strong. Becky needed to work at being more independent by exploring her own needs and desires.

Do you ever feel like you can't be yourself? That you say what others want to hear rather than what you truly believe? You might feel like a phony, like you're not being honest, because you're unsure of whether to speak your mind. Do you find yourself giving in to others and not standing your ground because you don't trust your own judgment? You could be so used to adapting to and agreeing with others that you really don't know how you honestly feel. It can be difficult to feel independent when you don't know what opinions and beliefs you represent. On the other hand, you might have a difficult time knowing when it's okay to change your mind, give in to, or agree with someone else? When this happens, you might feel rigid about insisting on having things your own way, and others may even call you stubborn. These are some questions that reveal the quality of your interpersonal boundaries, as well as the structure of your identity and the integrity of your relationships.

In adolescence, the search for identity is primary. Teens try out new attitudes, as well as new clothing styles and groups of friends, in order to create their personal comfort zone of identity. But in reality the development of identity continues throughout life, well into adulthood. Your social identity is unique and defines who you are to the world. It evolves and changes over time based on your life experiences in combination with your innate temperament.

Identity is expressed both internally, in your feelings and thoughts, as well as externally through your actions. Ideally, a strong, well-defined identity grounds you and gives you a feeling of safety and security as you interact in the world. You know who you are and who you aren't, because you have integrity, an authentic and genuine way of presenting yourself to the world. Without a strong identity, you are either overly influenced by others or detached and self-absorbed. Have you noticed that you feel most comfortable when your thoughts, feelings, and actions match? The more they vary, when you change with different people and in different circumstances, the more out of sync you feel. It feels good when you can be genuine wherever you go with whomever you meet. This includes letting others know what you believe and stand for; trusting your ability to evaluate information that you receive and use it to make good decisions; and being willing to give as well as take in relationships.

The place where your identity stops and makes contact with the identity of another person is called your interpersonal boundary. This is the place where the needs of one person end and the needs of the other person begin. Think again of the example of the sand and ocean; the point where the sand and the ocean meet and where their differences become evident is their point of contact. Your ability to achieve balance, at the point of this boundary, between your own needs and the needs of others, determines how successfully you will interact socially and also influences the quality of your relationships. Healthy boundaries are based on integrity and promote mutually beneficial relationships, while unhealthy boundaries breed exploitation and dysfunction. In order to have successful interpersonal relationships, it is essential that you live an authentic life that includes balanced interpersonal boundaries. Humans are social beings and integrity in relationships is essential for healthy and mutually productive coexistence.

G: Genuine and Authentic discusses the four steps to living an authentic lifestyle: Know What You Stand For, Live in Your Circle of Integrity, Handle External Pressures, and Make Ethical Choices. You will learn what it takes to live a life in which what you feel, what you think, and what you do are in harmony with one another. The exercises in this section will help you experience the feeling of staying firm and true to yourself which happens when you don't allow others to pull you away from thinking, feeling, or doing what is important to you. You will live with integrity when you know who you are, know what you believe, and own it.

G
Being in Your Circle Experience

Imagine that you are standing in a room with your feet firmly planted on the ground. Picture a circle drawn around you about as far away from you as you are tall. Or, imagine your circle in another way, by stretching your arms, one at a time, out in front of you. Sweep each arm across your body and then out to your side as far as you can comfortably reach while standing straight. Turn around and sweep each arm once again. Either way you choose to create your imaginary circle, it will be just the right size for you.

Imagine that this circle defines your personal boundary, establishing the division where your identity ends and that of the rest of the world begins. Next, imagine this circle filled with all the traits and attributes, skills, and interests that describe you. In addition, add to your circle your beliefs and expectations, as well as your opinions about the world. For example, you might believe that people ought to be kind to one another or that having fun is necessary, or that you should vote in every political election or live green.

Hint: One variation is to imagine your circle being filled with brightly decorated presents, each representing one of your unique traits. Another variation is to imagine your circle filled with pictures or snapshots of you doing those activities that you most value about yourself or fulfilling the dreams and desires that you most want to achieve. No matter how you envision your circle, fill it with all that is you, all the things you can embrace and take in about you!

Close your eyes and take several deep breaths while you imagine standing in the center of all that describes who you are and what you believe. Feel the power of knowing that you are surrounded by all that is familiar. Feel the energy grow inside you as you experience your inner strength and your knowledge of self.

G: Genuine and Authentic

Step One: Know What You Stand For

Susan B. Anthony, leader of the women's suffrage movement, epitomized a person whose actions and words were consistently in alignment with her beliefs. She stayed true to her conviction that women should be equal to men under the law and dedicated her entire life to this cause. Her success was based upon her confidence, her integrity, and her single-minded commitment to this cause.

Living with integrity means that what you think, what you say, and what you do are synchronized. Individuals who have integrity know what they stand for and own it. They live authentic lives. Think of some individuals you know or have heard about who embody integrity. Perhaps someone like Susan B. Anthony, Martin Luther King, Jr., Amelia Earhart, Jimmy Carter, Gandhi, or Eleanor Roosevelt comes to mind. All of these individuals expressed unwavering beliefs with passion and commitment. Or perhaps you know of someone in your own family or group of friends who lives in an authentic manner, someone who is genuine, honorable, and reliable. A worldwide audience isn't necessary for an individual to have an impact on those around him. There are many people in the world who have this hard-to-define quality that causes others to trust their words, try to model their actions, and believe in their causes. We are drawn to persons with integrity because of their solid, unwavering beliefs and principles. They know who they are and they know what they stand for.

So how does one build integrity? The first step is to know and recognize the combination of traits and characteristics that are uniquely yours, which are the components of your identity. Think of your identity as an imaginary circle that surrounds you. It outlines your space and defines where you begin and where you end. It includes all of the **elements** that describe who you are, such as intelligent, social, political activist, avid snow skier, and the other elements you identified in previous chapters. For example, you may believe men and women are equal, there is life after death, people need to help one another, and so on. The contents of your circle also include your actions, choices and preferences, such as deciding to become a teacher, preferring Middle Eastern food, choosing to live in a condo rather than a single-family home, and others. The challenge in identifying the elements in your circle lies in first discovering, then knowing, and finally owning and living true to your authentic way of being.

The size of your circle is important, too. Please recall the initial exercise in this chapter, *Being in Your Circle Experience,* and the circle you generated. Now imagine your circle is smaller. To experience this, fold your arms and hold them close to your chest. See how your sphere of influence has shifted and narrowed. How can you connect with your world when you can't even reach out? You can't because you need a comfortable range; you need some breadth.

When your circle is too large, on the other hand, you feel off center and imbalanced. To feel this, stretch your arms out once again in an arc but strain to reach out, bend forward on tiptoes to get every inch that you can. What does that feel like? Chances are you feel awkward, like you've lost your balance. That's what it's like when your circle is too large, when you're stretching to include elements in it that don't comfortably fit. You're over-reaching your boundaries. Keep these images in mind as we continue our discussion of what it's like to honor your circle.

When you make decisions and choices that are consistent with your identity, and which are genuine reflections of your personal belief system, you stay in your circle and behave in an authentic manner. You are being true to yourself when you act with integrity and feel confident about who you are. If, however, you attempt to acquiesce and conform to external controls, when doing so is not consistent with your values, then you are not acting with integrity, and you feel off balance and pulled out of your circle.

Paula was considering where to spend the upcoming Thanksgiving holiday weekend. She was expected to be at her parents' home with the extended family. Paula, however, was also invited to spend the weekend with some girlfriends in Florida. Paula felt due for a no-stress holiday with friends, yet Paula hated to disappoint her mother. Paula took several deep breaths and found her circle. Within it, she recognized that she was a traditional type of daughter who was close to her mother and enjoyed family time. She was also a bit of a workaholic and her current feeling of overwork was due to this trait. In her circle, she also found a fun-loving, spontaneous spirit that was definitely underused. Some regret emerged at not attending the family dinner, yet some hope and a feeling of release emerged as she thought of fun-filled days on the beach with her best girlfriends. She decided to call her mom, explain her decision to go to Florida, and hope her mom would understand. This was a hard choice for Paula but one that allowed her to stay in her circle.

When you make decisions from your circle of integrity and authenticity, they may feel right to you but can involve making hard choices, some of them big, others small but meaningful. You might have to disappoint people who are close to you in order to do something beneficial for yourself. You choose whether to please someone else or to do something that feels right for you. This isn't being selfish; you're supporting your needs and authentic choices.

The content of your circle is not likely to change dramatically over time, but it is also not static. It is possible for you to discontinue behaviors that don't work and withdraw from people and places that no longer feel good. At one point in time following the Grateful Dead may have resonated with your belief about or passion for independent thinking and personal rights. Later in life, that type of connection may have passed or diminished in intensity, or it may have transferred to a career in human rights activism.

In the movie, Gran Torino, the main character played by Clint Eastwood, was very much a loner living firmly in his beliefs about how people should live. He was hardworking, honest, private, and independent. Other people's ways annoyed him and he had little tolerance for other's beliefs, customs, or ethnicity that differed from his own. He viewed the world in a black and white way. Later in the movie, through a series of events he began to extend his "circle" to seeing others who were racially different from himself in a new and positive way.

As shown in the previous example, you can add new elements to your circle that enhance and improve it because your belief system changes as you mature and acquire more life experiences.

> Jackie usually agreed with decisions her husband made for the family; however, when she entered graduate school, she felt more confident and formed more of her own opinions. This resulted in a greater willingness to provide input into family decisions. Her circle was expanding because she was becoming more aware of her identity and what was important to her, and so her choices were changing.

Modifications in traits, interests, and opinions are possible as you mature and grow because change is a natural part of life.

Charge Up Your Life Exercise One
Know What You Stand For!

Learn more about your beliefs and personal identity by doing the exercises below:

1. List the traits you are most proud of: your special talents, core values, political beliefs, and spiritual beliefs, as well as views on education, human rights, and the environment.

_____

_____

_____

2. Using the information in #1, compose a personal identity statement. For example, *I am Jane Smith, and I am intelligent, kind, caring, and love the outdoors. I value all living creatures and devote my free time to taking care of injured animals.*

_____

_____

_____

_____

G: Genuine and Authentic

Step Two: Live in Your Circle of Integrity

Taylor doesn't enjoy listening to jazz music or going to jazz clubs, so she regularly declines invitations to go. Gemma doesn't enjoy scary movies but she does enjoy love stories. Preferences can have qualifiers as well, such as Betsy loves good mystery books and movies, but not when the story involves trauma to a child such as in the film *Sophie's Choice* or in the television series *Law and Order Special Victim's Unit*. All of the preferences noted here are not inherently right or wrong. They are just right or wrong for these people. The important thing is to support your preferences and live in your personal circle of integrity.

When you are making decisions from your authentic place you feel calm, strong, centered, balanced, proud, clear, certain, confident, stable, joyful, and safe. It feels good to make decisions from your circle because your circle is a comfortable place to be. Living authentically feels right because you are being true to your essence, your inner core. When you feel in charge of yourself, the choices you make are conscious ones; you weigh all the alternatives and know that you are making decisions that come from your circle, your true self.

Think of your circle as your comfort zone, the place where things feel good to you. It isn't a place of extremes or judgments; what feels good to one person can feel bad to another. When you make decisions from your circle you are visible; other people can see the essence of who you are. At times, you may want to fit in and might have difficulty owning your beliefs and being clear in expressing them. Fear and shame can step in and interfere with your willingness to be visible, open, and honest. You might be afraid that if someone sees the real you and rejects you, you will not be able to endure the shame that accompanies the rejection. Think about the child in elementary school who disrupts the math class because he can't do the work. Being chastised for his misbehavior is preferable to letting the teacher and his classmates see what the real problem is, that he can't do the math and feels ashamed. Can you think of a situation where you were fearful of being exposed? Can you identify the real source of your shame?

Also, there may be times when you know what you want but you make a choice to do something else, such as accepting a job which allows you to be home for your kids. The difference is that you are choosing to do this, which indicates that you are living inside your circle. You are visible with this choice and your reasons for doing it. For the future, you know that when the kids can be more independent, you'll pursue your dream job.

Examine the choices you make during your day about what you think and believe, how you feel and what you do. They can be simple decisions like what you ate for breakfast, the clothes you wore, the calls you returned, the decision to work out in the evening, or they can be more important decisions like what car to purchase, or where to spend the upcoming holiday. Assess whether these choices are genuine and authentic reflections of your unique self. Are you in your circle of integrity?

Change for the better happens when you practice living in your circle in small ways every day and notice the satisfaction you feel inside. Living in your circle is not about having your own way and being selfish. One time you may stand your ground and insist on doing what you feel is best for you, regardless of whether others disagree, and another time you may acquiesce to someone else's needs, but both choices result from a conscious, centered orientation. Living in your circle isn't about agreeing or disagreeing, per se. It's about choosing your response and expressing it from a centered, balanced place.

Staying in your circle can also be difficult if society's message is in opposition to your best interests. For instance, some people may stay in conflicted or abusive relationships because society tells them that it is preferable to be in any relationship than to be alone or that perhaps this is the best relationship that will come along, so be grateful for what you have. When singles think this way, they are out of their circle. They are influenced by factors outside of themselves and are not hearing their healthy inner voice. In business, statements such as "Do whatever it takes" or "The end justifies the means" can cause individuals to engage in practices which erode their integrity and place themselves in undesirable circumstances. Shame over not following the crowd can prevent you from living in your circle and being true to yourself.

When you are visible, your heart is open and you are passionate about your beliefs. This can be uncomfortable if you are advocating an opinion that isn't shared by your group; however, expressing your opinions and being true to yourself will bring you the greatest satisfaction. Others don't have to agree with you. Simple self-expression is the goal. When you live inside your circle you put yourself in places and situations where you'll be appreciated and comfortable, such as you'll choose a job where your talents are showcased and your coworkers are friendly and supportive.

Charge Up Exercise Two
Live In Your Circle of Integrity!

Practice living in your circle of integrity by doing the following:

1. One way to practice voicing your inner circle beliefs, values, and preferences is to use the <u>0-2 Response Check</u>, which is a fun way to keep yourself aware of your circle of integrity. When you express your opinion and speak up for yourself, you earn 1 point. When others agree with you or validate your opinion, you earn 2 points. If, however, you don't say anything and are silenced by fears, shame, and insecurity you earn 0 points. For example, if your friends suggest going to a horror movie and you don't like to go to violent or scary movies, you earn 1 point if you express your preference, you earn 2 points if your friends decide to choose another movie, or 0 points if you go along with the group and repress your needs.

2. Practice paying attention to and knowing what you want ahead of an anticipated event. For example, if you're going on vacation with family or friends, take time to think ahead of places you'd like to see, foods you would like to eat, or ways in which you would like to spend your time. Planning ahead will better prepare you for taking care of your needs when situations come up unexpectedly and you find yourself pulled out of your circle of integrity.

3. Can you think of a time when you were tempted to leave your circle of integrity, to do something that was not in your best interest? Describe that experience. In what ways could you change that experience to be true to yourself and remain in your circle?

4. How Much Time Do You Spend in Your Circle?

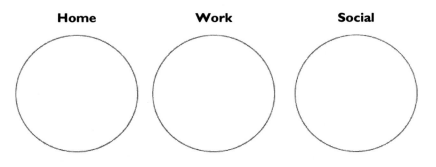

Home   **Work**   **Social**

a. For this exercise, you'll need a sheet of paper and some crayons, markers, or colored pencils. Draw three circles on the paper, side by side, and label them Home, Work and Social. Choose a different color to represent the four basic feelings: happy (comfortable, satisfied, joyful), sad (depressed, withdrawn, fatigued), angry (upset, frustrated, irritable), and scared (anxious, worried, insecure). Make a pie chart in each circle to indicate how often you feel each emotion in each of these settings. For example, if you feel happy half of the time at work, color half of the work circle in the color you chose to represent happy, and so on.

b. Next, think of situations in each setting that have generated each feeling and jot them down next to that section in your circles. For example, when you are at work, you might feel happy when your firm acquires a new client through your efforts. Think of examples for each of the feelings in each of the settings.

c. Now look at the charts you've created. Are your feelings in balance with how you want to feel in each part of your life? Are you satisfied with the outcomes? Can you see how often you feel each emotion in each setting? Do you feel a particular emotion in one setting more than another? Remember that when you are in your circle, you have positive feelings and when you are out of your circle, you have negative feelings.

d. What can you do to increase your time in your circle in each of these settings? Can you think of any ways you could decrease the negative feelings and increase the positive feelings you get in each of the settings? This transition from negative to positive will help you to connect to your authentic self, knowing that what you think, say, and do are in harmony. In what parts of your life are you living out of balance?

G: Genuine and Authentic

Step Three: Handle External Pressures

Hillary wanted to be accepted into her new upscale, trendy neighbor-hood. She shopped where her neighbors shopped, embraced their opinions, hired decorators they suggested, and tried to model them in as many ways as possible. She wanted to belong but the energy this took was exhausting. Hillary just wanted to be happy; however, she was anything but. Instead, Hillary was stressed and anxious. She needed to find her circle and develop her own style rather than worry about pleasing her neighbors.

Some events and situations can pull you out of your circle leaving you feeling disoriented and out of control. Have you ever blown up a balloon and let it go so it flies all over the place? Have you ever felt like that erratic balloon, as if you have no direction or inner guidance? Or consider how a sailboat moves without a centerboard and rudder. It moves at the whim of the wind with no control over the direction it takes. Being out of your circle is like the balloon and the sailboat, which may leave you feeling unbalanced, confused, and lacking in confidence. You may find yourself angry or worried about what others think.

There are several ways in which you can be pulled out of your circle. First, the triggers you identified in A: **Accept Your Possibilities** can become buttons people push to take you out of your circle.

Recall the story of Joyce, who was criticized by her mother for being assertive as a child. As an adult, when others referred to her as assertive, she sometimes felt shame, a reminder of this issue from her past. This feeling of shame at times caused Joyce to try to appear non-assertive, which took her out of her circle. Being out of her circle, and not being true to herself, was uncomfortable. Joyce was a strong and independent person. She found herself weighing the alternatives of staying in her circle, and owning her ability to be assertive - against her desire to please others. Joyce understood when this was happening, and she tried hard to maintain her boundaries and stay focused on being her best self within her circle.

Second, ads can be triggers because they tap into your emotions and may cause you to experience BIG feelings. To illustrate this, consider some of the ads that you see promising the perfect job, weight, or lifestyle, such as the milk ad showing celebrities with the trademark milk moustache, or ads for a particular make of luxury car or brand of clothing. Ads such as these are designed to evoke longing for the product because the ad associates the product with your desire for love, happiness, and success. The models appear perfect and carefree; life is good for them because they own the advertised product.

For instance, if you buy into the idea that dressing fashionably is important, your BIG feelings for the desired outcome could tempt you into throwing out perfectly good clothes because they are no longer in fashion. You'll think "I'll be happy if I wear this brand of jeans." You may recall thinking that if you wore a certain suit or bought a certain beautiful dress, that you would be magically transformed into your idealized self, rather than being who you are. There's a difference between using fashion to dress appropriately and to feel comfortable, and letting fashion use you by tapping into your emotions.

A third way you are pulled out of your circle is by feeling responsible for people and issues that don't need to concern you. These feelings often arise from guilt. Knowing how to distinguish between what concerns you and what is about someone else helps you to keep healthy boundaries.

Anthony related well to his dad, but his brother John didn't. Whenever there was a conflict brewing between John and their dad, John begged Anthony to help smooth the issue over. Anthony felt uncomfortable doing so, but he felt guilted into being the intermediary. Anthony was upset and anxious when his father and brother were angry at each other, clear indicators that he was out of his circle. His guilt caused him to feel responsible for helping them to get along, instead of recognizing that their relationship was their responsibility and not his. When he was able to see that he was out of his circle, Anthony worked to maintain healthier interpersonal boundaries with both his dad and brother. Then Anthony felt better about interacting with both of them. He was able to stand back and offer suggestions when asked, but he didn't shoulder the responsibility by actively intervening with these two very important people in his life.

A fourth way you can be pulled out of your circle is by making choices that do not reflect your true self in order to please others.

At work, Ron reported that he supported his advertising team on a particular ad campaign, although he believed that parts of it could be offensive to certain groups. This caused considerable distress for Ron when he was called upon to support the campaign publicly. The values represented in this campaign were not in sync with Ron's circle; his integrity was compromised by stating his support.

Ron was pulled out of his circle when he made a decision that opposed his core beliefs. This is different from compromising, when both sides agree but neither party gives up their core values. You can get pulled out of your circle when your circle becomes so large, from incorporating other people's wishes and beliefs, to the point that you no longer recognize your own circle. You can also be pulled out of your circle by following people and groups who don't match your values. Saying that you believe in something that you don't is a lie that will gnaw at you from the inside, and the price you'll pay is a physical one.

Mercedes was a college student who ended her relationship with her longtime boyfriend Ken because she knew he did not share her values. She was attracted by his charisma, decisiveness, and spontaneity, qualities that she did not see in herself. She felt that allying with Ken gave her some of his allure, but it was an illusion. She recognized that she had generally been outside her circle in the relationship in order to please him and stay together. Mercedes had cut classes and distanced herself from good friends he did not like. She disregarded her values about academic achievement and loyalty to friends to remain with Ken, but over time, Mercedes did not feel centered, focused, or balanced with the choices she had made. Mercedes needed to find her own circle, and stop straining to include Ken's values in hers. Borrowing someone else's values never works.

Finally, at times you may meet people who are filled with self-interest and who cannot see the perspective of anyone but themselves. We label pathologically self-interested people sociopaths or narcissists, and thankfully they are rare; however, the people we are referring to are found everywhere in society in all occupations and all ways of life. They understand right and wrong, but simply set the concept aside in order to meet their own needs. One could be the coworker who never seems to have enough money for lunch, and who never pays you back when you lend him the difference. Another could be the friend who can never drive because she always seems to be low on gas. Yet another could be the charming business associate who always seems to make money on projects while you take a loss.

When you encounter these people, if at all possible, move away from them. They aren't apt to change and, over time, you'll feel bad about yourself, since they will subtly but surely undermine your self-esteem. When you cannot sever the relationship, it is important for you to stand your ground, express yourself respectfully, using the 0-2 Response, but firmly, and refuse to be exploited.

Generally, you are out of your circle when you value someone else's opinion more than your own. Recognize when you are letting your emotions overrule your good sense. Integrity is an inside-out process that involves checking in with who you are at your essence and making decisions that are authentic. Staying in your circle can at times be challenging and involve making hard choices, but the end result is worth it.

Charge Up Your Life Exercise Three
Handle External Pressures!

When is your circle too small and closed off to others? And when is it too large, reaching into others' lives? Try the following exercises to find out:

1. Think of a time, situation, or relationship when your circle was too small, closing others out — when you were rigid, inflexible, and controlling? Write your experiences in the first column below.

2. When was your circle too large and you lost sight of what was your responsibility and what was someone else's? Recall a time when you lost track of your circle, tried to please others at your own expense, and were pulled out of it. Write your experiences below in the second and third columns.

Circle Too Small Closing Others Out	Circle Too Large Reaching into Others' Lives	Out of Circle Pulled Out of Own Beliefs and Values
Ex: Stubbornly refused help from colleagues in completing my project.	Ex: Finished my child's homework assignment so she wouldn't have to deal with the consequences.	Ex: Took a ride from a coworker even though he had been drinking, and avoided confronting him.

G: Genuine and Authentic

Step Four: Make Ethical Choices

Jack, a corporate accountant, miscalculated the figures on an important project, and the difference in data was critical in a company decision. The data he presented indicated that his company stood to gain if they followed through on a project. Jack, however, was a meticulous professional, and in reviewing his data, he uncovered information that totally skewed the results in the opposite direction. If he said nothing, and maintained his standing as a professional with an impeccable reputation for precise accounting, his company might never uncover his error but would surely suffer in the future. If he spoke up, he ran the risk of exposing himself as flawed. Jack took pride in his reputation and had difficulty admitting that he could make mistakes. Jack had an ethical decision to make. He weighed the alternatives of his decision and assessed who would be helped and who would be harmed by it. Integrity overrode his need to appear faultless, and he reported the new data to his employer. This decision enabled Jack to see himself as a whole person, one who can make mistakes and own up to them.

Decisions like Jack's are difficult ones to make, but they define you as an ethical individual who recognizes that what you say and do does matter. Being authentic means that what you think, what you say, and what you do are in harmony. It involves honestly expressing your own value system without lying and cheating. This means that other people are able to count on your actions matching your words. If you say you are going to do something then you do it. When you are asked your opinion about an issue by more than one person, each person receives the same answer. Your personality has a seamless quality to it. This does not mean that you behave exactly the same everywhere, but that instead you consistently stand by your beliefs and live with integrity in a circle that is right-sized. It is possible for your circle to be too small, and when this happens, you might manipulate others for your personal benefit. It's also possible for your circle to be too large, which happens when you take care of everybody else at your own expense, and the line between the needs of self and others gets blurred.

You might wonder if it is okay to lie and cheat sometimes, like if a clerk gives you too much change or you discover a way to cheat on your taxes. Is there a test to determine how much honesty is necessary, and is it always unethical to lie? We can all think of little white lies we might tell, like complimenting your good friend on a new hairdo that isn't particularly becoming. But embellishing the truth because it sounds better or saying whatever is necessary to impress your audience is different, isn't it? Also, at times you may find yourself in a group of unethical individuals where the norm could be to take what you can get and get as much as possible for yourself. Continuing to stay with this group can erode your integrity and your good feelings about yourself. Think back to the 0-2 Response Check in situations such as these. If you don't feel validated by the group for your personal beliefs, maybe it's time to change groups.

An ethical decision could be uncomfortable for you, such as when you admit you were wrong, when you change your mind after acquiring new information, or when the conclusion that you draw will cause you to give up on something that has been important to you. The amount of resentment you feel after making a choice is a clue to whether or not the choice was authentic.

When you deviate from authenticity, you ruminate and second-guess your decisions. You resent the people who you feel made you move out of your circle. You feel pulled by them to do or say things that you cannot fully own. Your resentment gnaws at you, crowding your thoughts and affecting your daily functioning. This is different from choosing to do something that you'd rather not but, when you weighed the alternatives, you realized the choice needed to be made. One generates anxiety and tension and the other is centered and balanced. Notice how you feel after making a decision. Are you left with any emotional residue? If so, examine it to see where it comes from. Did you adopt someone else's values as your own? Did you step out of your circle? An authentic choice leaves no emotional residue. The choice could have been a hard one, but you would feel good having made it. Remember the examples of the sailboat and the balloon. Notice when similar feelings arise and consciously step back into your Circle.

> Tim's wife Angie enjoyed sailing and the couple purchased a small boat for weekend sails on a nearby lake. Angie looked forward to the outings and felt that Tim did also. Tim, however, hoped for rain every weekend and was dismayed when he woke to find the sun shining brightly. He had never been a water person and although he was a capable swimmer he did not enjoy water sports and was actually afraid of the water. His desire to please his wife and share time with her on the weekends overrode his need to do something he would enjoy more such as tennis, hiking, or even mowing the lawn! As the weeks went on Tim experienced nagging headaches that started earlier and earlier in the week and that, over time, he couldn't ignore. He agonized over the conversation he knew he had to have with Angie. When he broached the subject, Angie laughed amiably and assured him that she could easily find a companion to sail with and that she was willing to balance her sailing weekends with ones that included activities they both enjoyed. Tim's headaches stopped almost immediately. Recalling the 0-2 Points discussed earlier, Tim earned 2 points for this interaction. He got his needs met and his wife supported him.

Notice recurring health issues and consider whether they are signals that you have been pulled out of your circle. Emotional imbalances are communicated through body talk, which you first read about in H: Here and Now. Body talk can range from vague aches and pains to more serious medical conditions, which force you to pay attention to yourself. When you spend too much time out of your circle, or if you strain to make your circle wider, your body communicates your distress to you in symptoms that eventually cause you to stop and take notice. Your body is saying, "What about me? Who's taking care of my needs?" Body talk shows that you took care of someone else's needs at your own expense. After all, if you're always taking care of someone else, then who is taking care of you? The answer is "no one" and that won't feel good or be healthy over time.

When you tell a lie your body sends you a message. This body talk could be a tightening in the jaw, flutters in the stomach or the start of a headache. Practice listening to it by doing a body check.

Say out loud what you are thinking, feeling, or planning to do, and see if it feels true in your gut, or whatever body part is your signal of truth. If it is authentic, your body will be calm; if it isn't authentic, your stomach will feel sour. That's your inner self cueing you to either stay the course or think again.

You can test your body talk by doing the following: Think of a food that you especially dislike and stand in front of a mirror and say out loud how much you like it, with a big smile on your face. For example, try saying, "I love liver and onions" or some other food you abhor. Say it again, this time with more emphasis and a bigger smile on your face. Are you aware of any stirrings in your body that signal you have just told a lie? In your authentic circle, liver and onions are not served! Now try it another way. Think of something you really enjoy eating. Maybe it's chocolate, pie, or a good steak. Now say out loud, "I hate steak" and see what happens in your body.

Once you start to pay attention to your body talk you'll notice it more and more. You'll notice when you are being pulled out of your circle by inauthentic actions, thoughts, or feelings. You'll notice when you are lying to yourself about whether you are living in sync with your values and standards and expressing your authentic self.

In summary, building integrity involves your obligation as a social being. Humanity is interconnected and so it follows that what you think, say, and do has a lasting effect on the world. You don't exist in isolation. Your decisions affect others, both those who are close to you, like family and friends, and those who exist around you in a broader social sphere. When you recognize that you are part of society and not secluded or cut off from those around you, it feels unethical to make a decision from your circle that would harm someone else.

Eaton, the owner of a local guitar-building company, related the story of a customer who brought in a guitar worth two hundred dollars for repairs that would have cost much more than that, and would not have added value to the instrument. Eaton inquired whether the instrument had sentimental value, and when the owner said "no" Eaton felt caught in an ethical dilemma. Could he accept the business and make the repair, without informing the customer about the value of the guitar? All of us experience dilemmas like Eaton's daily. You may feel that the decision to accept the business was *a small one that didn't involve any great breach of integrity. After all, it's simply "doing business." But where do our responsibilities to our fellow human beings begin and those to us end? It's easier to make the "ethical" choice when the other person involved is a friend or a family member, but should we abdicate responsibility when the other person is a stranger or someone we will never encounter again? What do we tell ourselves so that we can proceed with only our interests in mind? Would Eaton be lying or cheating if he accepted the business? If Eaton lied by omission just leaving out important information, is that better?*

Decisions like Eaton's have an impact on all of us because we are interconnected social beings. When others act without integrity, it erodes our trust in humanity in general, far beyond Eaton. The litmus test is whether our actions result in harm to others, not just to our friends and family, but to humanity as a whole.

Your circle of integrity operates with standards and principles, barriers against wrong actions that can contribute to the demise or downfall of another person or group. Sometimes you need to make hard decisions, and others can feel uncomfortable or even outraged by them if they disagree. If you make those decisions from your principles, and they are a reflection of your best self, then you need to honor them. When you live authentically you are living within your circle, your genuine place of being. You stay present with what is actually happening at any point in time and recognize that your identity is a composite of traits, all of which you value and use appropriately. You work on communicating with respectful intentions and consideration for others. You form your own opinions, but you remain open to new information that could affect or even change your opinions. You express yourself with confidence. Your behaviors are a display of principled actions. You are aware of your needs and balance them with those of others and of the common good.

If you find yourself minimizing the effect of a simple ethical decision, consider the effect of a pebble tossed in a lake. The ripple continues far beyond where you can see. Ethical behavior has far-reaching effects because of the interconnectedness of our world. Be an agent of change by staying in your circle. Balance is the key because your personal decisions affect individuals as well as society as a whole.

Charge Up Exercise Four
Make Ethical Choices!

Explore your ethical beliefs in the following activities:

1. Where do you draw the line? Consider the following list of situations and determine where you draw the line on each one. Mark an "N" next to the issue that you think is Never acceptable to do under any circumstances. Mark an "O" next to the issues that you think are all right to do Occasionally. Mark an "A" that you think are Always acceptable to do.

____ Cheating on your taxes? For example, it's ok because government takes too much or government is too big.

____ Politicians taking money from lobbyists? For example, it's ok because it's legal.

____ Bait and switch deals on merchandise?

____ Multiple pages of legalese about your credit card that consumers can't understand?

____ Cutting in line?

____ Lying on your resume?

____ Walking away from a purchase with too much change?

____ Changing the labels on an item to pay a lower price?

____ Shoplifting?

____ Taking your neighbor's newspaper off their driveway?

_____ Hit and runs?

_____ Drinking and driving?

_____ Teachers taking gifts from students' parents?

_____ Companies taking water from public lands and then selling it?

_____ Environmental issues like fishing for whales or chopping down rainforests?

_____ Public smoking?

_____ Parking in a handicapped zone?

_____ Taking a newspaper from a vendor and not paying for it?

_____ Taking office supplies from work?

2. What are your pet peeves?

Notice your pet peeves about people or society in general. List them below. Do you notice a pattern? What underlying beliefs result in these judgments? For example, "I hate it when someone yells at their kids in public" which is based on my underlying belief that children should be respected. Or, "I hate it when people drink and drive" which is based on my underlying belief that we all need to contribute to a safe environment.

I hate it when people _____

I hate it when someone _____

3. What sayings do you use to justify unethical behavior? Look at the following list and write "Yes" if you've used these words or "No" if you haven't by each one. What other ones can you think of?

_____ It's about them not me.

_____ The end justifies the means.

_____ It's just good business.

_____ It's a dog eat dog world.

_____ A good offense is the best defense.

_____ Do whatever it takes.

_____ Take what you can get.

_____ My favorite charity is me.

Charge Up Your Life Milestones

G: Genuine and Authentic

Now that you have finished G: Genuine and Authentic, what skills have you learned and what ones are you still working on?

- Put a check mark in front of the statements that feel true to you right now.
- Mark a circle in front of the statements that you have not yet achieved.

_____ I understand who I am and what makes up my "circle."

_____ I balance my needs with those of others while maintaining my own integrity.

_____ My actions are authentic expressions of my true thoughts and feelings.

_____ Shame and embarrassment signal that I value someone else's opinion more than my own.

_____ I recognize that my extreme reactions are areas for potential growth.

_____ My body talk signals when I'm not being genuine.

_____ Generally, what you see is what you get with me.

_____ I respectfully speak my truth, rather than worry about pleasing others.

_____ I don't believe everything I'm told.

____ I can accept comments and advice that are important for my personal growth.

____ I recognize when fear of failure holds me back from reaching for a goal.

____ I understand that fear of success keeps me stuck in old patterns of behavior.

____ I'm working using "G: Genuine and Authentic" in the following ways:

_____

_____

_____

_____

_____

_____

_____

_____

_____

_____

_____

_____

_____

_____

_____

G – Genuine and Authentic

Additional Resources

The following is a list of suggested materials to help you on your journey to living an authentic life:

* *Getting Real: Ten Truth Skills You Need to Live an Authentic Life* by Susan Campbell, Ph.D. – offers a set of awareness practices to help you to let go of shoulds and find your authentic voice.

* *The Sociopath Next Door* by Martha Stout – outlines the markers of sociopathy which may be found in those closest to you.

* *I'm OK, You're OK* by Thomas Harris – discusses how the roles we play and our underlying motivations determine our actions and, consequently, what happens in the future.

* *Creative Process in Gestalt Therapy* by Joseph Zinker – explains the rules, principles, aims, and methods of Gestalt therapy.

* *Being Genuine: Stop Being Nice, Start Being Real* by Thomas d'Amsenbourg – outlines practical skills to allow you to remove the masks which are barriers to intimacy and connections.

* *Moral Politics: How Liberals and Conservatives Think* by George Lakoff – explains how the underlying philosophy of each political group guides their decision making.

"You'll always
be in fashion
when you're true
to yourself."

———*Maya Angelou*
American Poet

E
Enjoy and Experience Life

Despair ◄────► Hope

- Notice Negativity
- Let Yourself Be Happy
- Hope and Dream
- Live in Harmony

"Connect to the world in a positive way."

"Optimism is the
faith that leads to
achievement.
Nothing can be
done without hope
and confidence."

—*Helen Keller*
American Author and Activist
(1880–1968)

E: Enjoy and Experience Life
Despair ←——→ Hope

Introduction

> Harry was feeling depressed and hopeless about his future. His job was in jeopardy and his home was in foreclosure. His wife and children were supportive yet he felt like a loser. Harry's wife checked out rental properties while he spent hours on the internet searching for jobs unsuccessfully. However, Harry did manage to connect with a group blogging about similar economic issues. Sharing made Harry feel as if he wasn't alone. As group members helped one another by sharing their ideas and expertise, Harry stopped feeling like a loser and started to feel more hopeful.

To be happy and avoid depression connect to your inner strength and joy by moving beyond the negative feelings that keep you stuck and discontented. The good news is that depression is a process that does not occur suddenly. Deep sadness and feelings of despair develop over time when they are allowed to continue unrecognized and unchecked. To avoid the pitfalls of depression recognize the signs of negative thinking and despair at the point when they can be managed, before they progress into depression. Becoming aware of the signs of unrelenting despair is the first step in heading it off and setting your life on a hopeful course. It is easier to intervene at the start of the cycle of depression than to wait until you have become debilitated and are experiencing serious dysfunction at home, at work, or in your social life.

Procrastination, fear of failure, fear of success, and addictive behaviors are ways to avoid happiness and allow negativity, and later despair, to enter your life. When you understand how these dysfunctional behaviors interfere with your life, you can move away from them and focus on being happy. There is enough love, happiness, and success to go around in the world, but you have to actively seek out your share of them and live with hope. Hope involves energy and movement.

E: Enjoy and Experience Life contains the four steps that illustrate what it means to think positively and avoid or relieve depression: Think Positive, Let Yourself Be Happy, Hope and Dream, and Live in Harmony. You will learn how to recognize negative thinking patterns and see how they affect your life. You'll practice thinking positively, building hope, and setting your life on a course to achieve your goals.

When you finish working through this final barrier, you will have all the tools necessary for your journey of personal growth. You'll understand that not only are you worthwhile just as you are, but you are also part of a greater whole, where your contribution is necessary and irreplaceable. You'll recognize that all human beings are connected to one another, and share a common desire for a joyful life. Only by reaching out and connecting in a meaningful and ethical way can you realize your full potential.

E
The World Market Experience

Imagine being in a market that sells items from countries throughout the world. Notice the vastness of this market and the variety of people shopping and working as well as the items that are for sale. Wander up and down the aisles and look at what each country offers. Notice the languages that you hear, some familiar and some not. What languages do you enjoy listening to? Notice the hustle and bustle of the market and hear the laughter of the children and the bartering and bantering of the adults.

Smell the aromas from the food tents, where you see people relaxing and enjoying a break as they eat and chat with one another. Taste some of the food samples as you amble down the aisles. Which tastes make you want more? Notice the textures, colors, and styles of clothing that people in each country wear. Which pieces are attractive to you? What would you like to try on? Enjoy the experience of shopping in this fascinating world market.

Now imagine the day is drawing to a close and the sun is beginning to set. It's time for you to go. One of the shopkeepers approaches you and offers to you an item that he holds in his hands as a gift meant specifically for you. As you look at it, you smile in delight and graciously accept it from him.

What is it? Think of an answer before you read on.

The gift that you imagine says something about you, what is important to you, what you seek out in times of need. For example, one woman imagined receiving a fur rug that she associated with warmth and comfort, feelings that she seeks out in times of anxiety or sadness. Another woman imagined a crystal globe that indicated to her that she sees possibilities in the world. A gentleman imagined receiving some food, which indicated to him a desire to be nurtured. What meaning does your gift have?

E: Enjoy and Experience Life

Step One: Notice Negativity

Marlon felt he was stuck at a dead-end job in his uncle's small printing company. Marlon was a talented graphic designer but he felt his skills were untapped in his current position. He was capable of doing more than designing envelopes, posters, and business stationery! Coming to work every day was getting harder and harder, but the thought of finding another position was equally unpleasant. He focused on the negative aspects of leaving such as his uncle's disappointment and his need to maintain medical benefits for his daughter's healthcare needs. Marlon's wife noticed that his despondency and negativity were filtering into their home life and personal relationship. She suspected that Uncle Pat was noticing his negative attitude at work too. She saw her husband moving down the road to despair, so she started a discussion with Marlon about either working on a more positive attitude or looking for a more satisfying job.

Do you ever find yourself stuck in a situation or relationship in which you have little or no control? Perhaps you've felt victimized by your work environment, your spouse, a friend, or an overpowering circumstance. Or, perhaps you've felt overwhelmed by situations that seem unmanageable and out of your control such as health issues, weight management, financial concerns, or family relationships. When you feel stuck in one of these ways, you might notice some patterns of negative or depressive thinking. For example, you might have a tendency to view the world in terms of what is missing or wrong, rather than in terms of what is right. You might have a tendency for filtering out the positives, making problems bigger than they need to be, thinking in black-and-white terms, and squelching the fun and enjoyment out of life. Negative thinking gone unchecked can lead you on the road to despair, where life becomes intolerable and unhealthy.

A young woman named Mia described it as being alone in a deep, dark, damp, narrow hole with tall sides opening at the top where a dim light illuminated her barren surroundings. She felt the way out was beyond her reach; there were no toe holds on the slippery sides, yet even if someone lowered a ladder down, she couldn't muster the energy to climb it. She wouldn't have the power to put her foot on the first rung.

Despair marks the low point in any person's life. If you have experienced despair, you will have no problem resonating with the feelings of passivity, hopelessness, and helplessness that are its hallmarks. Despair is the end result of a long process of detachment from self and others that undermines your functioning at home, at work, and in social situations. The good news is that despair doesn't happen quickly and can often be stopped by becoming aware of the signs and taking steps to change to a more positive course.

It is true that you perceive the world through your own personal filter and that no one thinks about you as much as you do. This often makes it difficult to take the perspective of someone else and see their point of view. However, on the road to despair, egocentric thoughts can take over your life and become habitual and pervasive. When you become acutely self-involved, and don't take the time to consider the perspectives and opinions of others, you disconnect from the world, and your sense of what is real and unreal becomes distorted.

The importance of staying connected to friends and family cannot be overemphasized because you are a social being and need others to survive. In the movie *Cast Away*, Tom Hanks' character resorted to painting a face on a volleyball and naming it to ward off social isolation. When you feel excluded, isolated, or detached socially, you eventually will experience some degree of despair. Your negative feelings can be directed outward such as in one of the many school or community shootings, or inward in self-destructive behavior, such as suicidal ideation or "cutting." On the road to despair you feel isolated from others and don't share your personal needs.

Can you recall a time you felt disconnected, left out, or isolated from others? What were the emotions you experienced? Perhaps you felt sad, fearful, hopeless, or angry? The specific incident doesn't need to be monumental because even brief and relatively inconsequential situations can leave you feeling utterly alone.

> Tasha recalled when she was the only one of her friends to stay in the dorm over the Labor Day weekend. Everyone had gone home for the holiday, and the only show Tasha remembered watching on TV was the Jerry Lewis telethon. She felt alone and isolated, like no one knew where she was or what she was doing. She had ceased to be a part of other people's lives and felt disconnected and a bit afraid. She could feel herself sink into a dark and lonely tunnel. Fortunately, Tasha was able to look ahead forty-eight hours and know that her dorm would be full of people once again, making her negative feelings short-lived. But can you imagine what it would be like to feel like that all day, every day, as if there was no hope?

When you detach from others, you lose contact with the energy that social interactions generate. You feel helpless, hopeless, and passive; negative thinking clouds your judgment. You filter out the positive aspects of your life; your critical voice gains power and becomes loud and insistent. A problem in one area of your life moves into others; for example, an issue at work affects your home life. Your objectivity becomes clouded, you feel singled out and victimized, and you say things like, "Everyone else's life is better than mine." You see no end in sight because you cannot access the personal resources necessary to change the problem situation. Over time negative thinking is toxic and kills the spirit. Without spirit, hope has no place to grow and life takes on a grim face.

There are three types of negative thinking you can experience: catastrophizing, filtering, and personalizing. Each can cause you to feel helpless and hopeless, the hallmarks of despair. As you read the following, identify the types of negative thinking you engage in so you can avoid the pitfalls of depression. When you pay attention to the signs of negative thinking you can intervene and head off depression which opens your life to an abundance of possibilities.

When you catastrophize you believe that situations are bigger than they really are and that they affect far more than they actually do. You see a problem in one area of your life as affecting all areas.

Corbin was involved in a quarrelsome ten-year marriage that had recently erupted into a bitter divorce. Corbin was a laid-back, congenial individual who was satisfied with his position as operations manager of a small, low-stress corporation. He worked a straight eight-hour day, which left him plenty of time to connect with friends and family after work. His wife, Gwen, in contrast was a go-getter. She worked as a sales rep for an international pharmaceutical company and her competitive spirit had yielded financial dividends as well as an ever-increasing territory to manage. The difference in Corbin and Gwen's personality styles was initially intriguing to them, but the increasing disparity between their incomes and lifestyles began to grate on Gwen. She began to criticize Corbin for his lack of motivation and his inability to keep up with her financially. Her fault-finding deteriorated into petty criticisms of his clothing, his friends, his choice of interests and his manner of speaking. Corbin loved his wife but felt helpless and powerless at home. He began to see himself as inadequate in general and because of this all areas of his life began to suffer. Corbin needed to recognize that this problem was finite; it only involved one area of his life and did not need to spread into his work and social life.

Separating areas of your life as much as possible during times of trauma allows you to feel more in control, which makes it easier for you to take charge of your life. Can you recall a situation that you made worse by catastrophizing? When events are magnified they create negativity because they seem overwhelming and impossible to solve. When they are perceived as "right-sized" they become manageable. Can you think of a time when you let a problem at work affect your home life, or when a problem at home affected your work?

The second type of negative thinking, filtering, leads you to view situations with pessimism, and you see only the worst and avoid the positive elements that could help you feel hopeful and keep situations in perspective.

Eddie anticipated that the coming holiday dinner would be ruined because he and his sister, Laurel, were involved in a conflict. Eddie focused too much on that one element and overlooked the fact that there would be other relatives attending the event that he would enjoy seeing. Filtering caused Eddie to divide this family event into black-and-white elements, which led him to view it in an all-or-nothing way.

Notice when you view events with a negative filter and minimize the positive. What feelings does this type of negative thinking create in you? You might feel sad, angry, or anxious. When you view events with a negative filter over time this creates negative mental pathways and habitually pessimistic interpretations of the world. In order to keep balanced and maintain a realistic outlook on your life, it's helpful to recognize both positive and negative aspects of a situation. When you catch yourself filtering, remind yourself to focus on the whole situation and not just the negative parts

Personalizing, the third type of negative thinking, originates from an egocentric point of view through which you feel that everything is all about you and that all events somehow relate to you. **Personalizing takes two basic forms:**

In the first form you perceive that events are happening to you alone and not to others; you might imagine that other people's lives are better or happier than yours. When you recognize that setbacks are impersonal, you realize that problems happen to everyone, that no one is immune. At times you may feel as though you are singled out and victimized; for example, in difficult financial times, families often lose jobs or homes, or become mired in debt. Staying present through the crisis allows the family to generate a plan for the future because hope, not despair, guides their actions.

In the second form of personalizing you view situations as being about you without checking them out, as you might do if a friend or colleague does not greet you enthusiastically, or doesn't have time to talk when you call.

> Olivia stopped speaking to her closest friend, Maxine, when she thought Maxine had ignored her. Maxine was busy at work because a huge deadline was looming. She had little time to eat, let alone spend time with friends and engage in other activities. Olivia called several times to ask Maxine to meet her for lunch; however, Maxine declined the invitations which made Olivia feel hurt and disregarded. Olivia isolated herself from her friend because the situation triggered her feelings of "I'm not good enough." Olivia's personal filter caused her to assume that this situation was about her. She failed to recognize that people's thoughts, feelings, and actions most often relate to themselves and to no one else. Anger soon grew and Olivia wrote Maxine a nasty email addressing Maxine's lack of concern for her and their friendship.

Olivia felt justified in her anger and belief that Maxine was not her good friend. Olivia personalized Maxine's behavior. Only after repeated conversations was Maxine able to repair the relationship and convince Olivia that she was mistaken. Olivia and Maxine's problem is an example of how simple issues can drive both personal and professional relationships apart.

Think of a time when you personalized an event and assumed it was about you, when perhaps it was not? Did you check it out to be sure that your impressions were accurate? Looking back at this situation, in what way could you have handled it differently?

Generally, negative thinking loses its power when you are hopeful and believe that setbacks are temporary and impersonal. What is happening now will pass because change is the most constant part of life. The most painful of events will either pass or will lose their intensity over time. Problems are more manageable when you don't allow them to affect all areas of your life. Taking action and feeling effective in making change is critical in combating negative thinking. Action generates energy, which keeps you in the present, where you can access resources and connect with your support system.

Consider the quality of your thinking patterns to determine how often you focus on the negative. Noticing your negative thinking patterns helps to ultimately destroy them. Being aware of the frequency and intensity of negativity is the first step in moving away from despair. Hint: you might put a coin in a jar or gently snap a rubber band around your wrist when you notice yourself thinking negatively. Spending more time seeking out positive connections with others will also help you stay hopeful and move you toward your goals and dreams.

Charge Up Exercise One
Notice Negativity!

Become aware of your negativity by doing the following exercises:

1. As you go about your day, catch yourself in negative or self-critical thoughts which cause you to feel helpless and hopeless. Notice the critical voice inside that tells you, for example, how unattractive you look today, how you'll never be able to get ahead, or how you don't compare well to others. What does your critical voice tell you? Make a list of your negative thoughts below.

2. Next, place an "X" by one of the three types of negative thinking: catastrophizing, filtering, or personalizing that best matches each item on your negative thought list.

	Negative Thought	Catastrophizing	Filtering	Personalizing
1.				
2.				
3.				
4.				
5.				

E – Enjoy and Experience Life

Step Two: Let Yourself Be Happy

Natalie noticed that her bedroom furniture was run down and cracked in several places. She and her husband decided to purchase a new bedroom set, this time one of better quality. They went to an exclusive furniture store and, after spending considerable time with a decorator, ordered some beautiful and expensive pieces. When the furniture finally arrived and was set up in their room, Natalie felt agitated and overwhelmed. She told her husband that she didn't like the furniture and wanted it sent back to the store. Her husband couldn't understand her intense reaction after they had spent so much time selecting just the right pieces. Natalie was not aware of the underlying reason that was driving her to return the furniture: Natalie came from a humble childhood and could not imagine herself with such elegance. Even though she now could afford such luxury, she did not feel she deserved it.

Do you believe that there is enough money, respect, influence, power, peace, harmony, friends, fame, possessions—or whatever it is you seek—to go around, and do you feel entitled to a share of them? Or do you have an inner voice that tells you that you're not good enough or smart enough to have these things? Does this negative voice tell you that you'll only be happy after you find a mate, after you lose weight, or when you finish that degree? Listening to this negative inner voice stops you from being happy because it holds you back from reaching out for the abundance that the universe has to offer. With the necessary skills needed to reach your goals, the only thing holding you back from having all that you seek is the belief that you don't deserve what you are seeking.

Fear of failure is another issue you may identify with that stands in the way of your happiness. You may worry about doing your best and still not achieve your goal, so one way to avoid failing is not to try at all. In Knowing Where You Are, the first step of H: Here and Now, we discussed that anxiety is fear of the unknown and it is generated when you ruminate over past experiences or feel apprehensive about the future. Anxiety does not exist in the present moment, so any time you feel fear, you are not present. When you fear failure, your thinking is either in the past or the future where no action takes place. Being frozen in fear, therefore, stands in the way of reaching your goals and attaining ultimate happiness.

Odd as it may seem, you can also have a fear of success. Consciously or unconsciously, you may wonder what you will do if you reach your goal. You may fear others will expect you to continue your achievement, and you may wonder if you will be able to keep up the pace that may be required. You may worry about making changes in routine, status, living arrangements, obligations, and time spent with family and friends that often accompany success. If you achieve your goal, you might also need to give up your negative outlook on life and accept the fact that you are a success. You would need to admit that there is enough success to go around for everyone, so your thinking would need to change. Both positive and negative changes can be intimidating. The thought of making change in the future can freeze you in place in the present. So, once again, fear of success is not about the present but about the future. When you fear success, because you fear the future, you actively avoid success, even while you insist that you are pursuing it.

Russell was seeking employment after he was laid off unexpectedly; however, he always seemed to have a reason why he didn't get his application in on time, or couldn't reach anyone to arrange for an interview, or why the job itself wasn't just right. He was setting himself up for failure. Russell was his own worst enemy. Just when he was on the verge of success, such as when someone gave him a good lead on a job, he made an about-face turning away from it, through his undermining actions. This was puzzling for his family and friends to watch, and perhaps even for Russell himself to experience. But all behavior is intentional. Every one of Russell's thoughts, feelings, and actions was purposeful and meaningful. Russell was actively avoiding success through his own actions and setting himself up for failure time and time again, because failure was what he believed he deserved.

Can you think of a time when you actively avoided success?

How did you undermine your chances for success? Is fear of success or feeling undeserving holding you back now?

Procrastination is another way you avoid happiness and success. Remember that procrastination is always intentional because it allows you to avoid moving to the next step. Notice when you delay or forget. Notice when you do things slowly or poorly. Notice when you find it hard to concentrate and pay attention to a task. If so, consider what it is you are avoiding and what would happen if you moved forward. Ask yourself if the goal is something you really want. If it is, then what is the fear causing you to delay acting? At times individuals who are close to you might criticize or mock you for pursuing a goal. Their intention is to subtly undermine your success out of envy or jealousy. They don't want you to achieve more than they have, or enjoy as much success in your life as they have in theirs. They might say they are keeping your best interests at heart, but if your goal is valuable to you, then your inner voice is the one that should be loudest in your ears.

Jim was a young man in his mid-twenties who was a chronically negative thinker. He had honed the ability to filter out the positive and focus on the negative down to a fine art. He felt unsettled, fatigued, and confused about his circumstances and came for help about a specific problem he felt helpless to overcome: for the last five years he had been two courses short of completing his bachelor's degree in accounting and so remained in a near-minimum-wage bookkeeping position and lamented his inability to move up in the company. Past history revealed that he was a bright young man but a consistent underachiever throughout his academic career. He could always find a reason why he couldn't finish his degree— the course wasn't offered, the professor was too difficult, the demands of his job were increasing, and so on. The conditions were never quite right for success. Discussion revealed that Jim was the only member of his family to ever attend college, let alone graduate. Throughout his life, his family had subtly undermined his intelligence. His relatives called him "college boy" and his dad had accused him of feeling he was better than or smarter than the rest of the family. This was a difficult situation to deal with, and Jim's procrastination was his remedy. How could he move ahead with his own goals without leaving his family, whom he loved, behind?

Once Jim recognized the origins of his procrastination, got in touch with his own needs, and gave himself permission to meet them, he would be on his way to success and happiness.

You might wonder whether there is a balance in the universe and whether you might have filled your quota for it because our culture sends self-limiting messages like "the bigger they are the harder they fall." This can cause you to fear what would come next, especially what would be taken away from you in retribution, if you got a little more in life; this follows the "what goes up, must come down" line of thinking. Possibly the universe could cut short your success just when you are enjoying it most. Fear of retribution could keep you from going after success in the first place. Know, instead, that you have a right to love, success, and happiness, just like everyone else.

Dreams, which we've discussed before, can be a great source of information about how you pursue goals and whether you set yourself up for success or failure. First, we looked at "water" in dreams as markers of your emotional status in the *Keep Situations Right-Sized* section of H: Here and Now. Next, we showed how "houses" in dreams can be an indication of how you judge yourself in the *Notice Every Trait* section of A: Accept Your Possibilities. Now, we'll look at how your dreams communicate your motivation to find love, happiness, and success. Consider the role that modes of transportation play in your dreams. Are there cars, trucks, buses, trains, bicycles? Do you walk instead? Do you get around in your dreams by yourself or in a group, such as on a bus? If you're in a car, are you the driver or the passenger? Are you in the backseat or the front seat? How does your vehicle work; for example, are the brakes in good condition? Do you reach your destination? What kind of interference do you encounter? All of these pieces in your dream tell you how you are feeling about your ability to reach goals and find success in your daytime life.

Tammy dreamed of driving alone in a small car that was running well. She rode along until she came to a steep hill and instead of continuing in her car, she parked it and began to walk up the hill, huffing and puffing with exertion. She walked partway up the hill and then turned around to look at her parked car. She wondered why she had decided to walk rather than stay in her car and simply drive up the hill. She walked back, got in her car and drove quickly to the top of the hill. This dream revealed that Tammy often made things harder for herself than she needed to. She missed out on important opportunities, which undermined her ability to meet her goals. She felt motivated and driven when she focused her efforts and maximized her opportunities. Assess your ability to meet your goals by becoming aware of what your dreams are trying to communicate to you about your drive and motivation.

Engaging in addictive behavior is yet another way you show that you do not deserve success. When you feel overwhelmed or undeserving of success and don't perceive that you have the resources to cope, you want the discomfort to go away now, not later, and addictions can be a quick fix. Addictions temporarily distract you from people or situations that you find troubling. They give you a false feeling of control. They can be as simple as excessive reading or TV watching, mindless shopping, obsessive cleaning, compulsive exercising, or engaging in poorly thought out relationships. Addictions can also be as serious as abuse of drugs or alcohol, excessive sex or food, shoplifting, or thrill-seeking. A behavior is addictive when you engage in it, chronically and repetitively, in order to avoid dealing with something in your life.

Emily watched re-runs of Law and Order every night, hour after hour, rather than deal with the fact that she needed to **look for work**. Wayne tinkered with his car for hours on end rather than focus on his deteriorating relationship with his wife. Paul hiked, played racquetball, and worked out daily for hours rather than deal with the fact that he needed to pay his bills.

Engaging in addictive behaviors is not the same as intentionally choosing to set aside a problem or demanding task for a time and doing something fun to take your mind off it. Notice how you escape. What purposeless activities do you find yourself engaging in to avoid paying attention to what is actually happening in your life?

In the middle of typing an important term paper, Victoria felt overwhelmed. She decided to take a break and arrange a number of boxes of family pictures into albums. The task was an intentional distraction from *the stress of typing and allowed her a much-needed break. After working on the pictures for several hours, she went back to typing with renewed energy.*

Intentional distractions give us a much-needed break from a demanding activity or situation. Addictive behaviors, in contrast, are ways to avoid dealing with whatever issues are before you because you perceive them as unmanageable. Notice how you distract yourself. Is it intentional and does it serve a purpose, such as giving you a break from something you find demanding or stressful? After the break, do you return to the activity with renewed energy? Or do you find yourself avoiding certain situations, people, or painful feelings by engaging in purposeless addictive behaviors? When you scratch the surface of an addictive behavior, chances are good that you will reveal negative thinking patterns. Although addictive behaviors may be effective at taking you away from your problems for a brief period, they are not adaptive or functional. They don't keep you balanced and don't help you to take charge of what is happening in your life. Addictions are useful in denying the problem, if only briefly, but the problem itself doesn't go away. It is simply delayed. How do you escape from your problems? How do you distract yourself? Is it intentional or addictive?

As you can see, the pursuit of love, happiness, and success, carries with it certain truths that may be hard to face. For example, if you want to find happiness, you need to give up unhappiness as a way of life. You need to reject your fear of finding happiness and achieving success. You need to believe that dreams can come true and that you are deserving of them. You need to believe that there is an abundance of love, happiness, and success in the world and that you are entitled to your share.

Charge Up Exercise Two
Let Yourself Be Happy!

Practice being happy by doing the following positive and enlightening activities:

1. Think of someone you know who you judge as happy or successful. What do you admire or envy about this person? Do you believe there is enough of what you envy for you to have a share? What is standing in the way of your having it?

_____

_____

_____

_____

2. If you had three wishes, what would they be? Are they realistic? What stands in the way of making each of your wishes come true? Do you need to acquire a skill or find a mentor? List all the reasons that you believe stand in the way of your reaching these goals.

_____

_____

_____

_____

3. Notice your addictive behaviors and what you are avoiding with thoughts such as, "Oh well, I might as well _____ (eat another cookie, go to the racetrack, watch TV all day)." Make a list of the activities that you do. Mark an "X" under Intentional if the activity is one you do purposefully to give yourself enjoyment or a break from another task. Mark an "X" under Avoidant if the activity distracts or diverts you from dealing with issues or problems. Keep on the lookout for addictive behaviors that have depressive thinking at their core.

Activity	Intentional	Avoidant
Watching favorite TV show	X	
All day Saturday TV		X

E: Enjoy and Experience Life

Step Three: Hope and Dream

Hannah recalled the birth of her first grandchild. Her body felt full to bursting with energy, and a smile crossed her face from ear to ear. Every cell in her body felt alive and stimulated. She felt better than good. She couldn't wait to spread the word. The birth of this baby symbolized hope for the future for Hannah and her family. What special event caused you to feel joy? Keep it in mind as you read on.

Emily Dickinson wrote, "Hope is the thing with feathers that perches in the soul." This familiar quote embodies the belief that hope involves energy and movement, and it also shows that hope grows within the soul, the essence of an individual, so connecting with your essence is necessary to feel hope. By reading the text and working through the exercises in the five earlier chapters of *Charge Up Your Life*, you have been practicing how to be present in your life. Learning how to nurture your preferences, relieve anxiety, accept all parts of yourself, communicate effectively, and set healthy interpersonal boundaries all helped you to get to know yourself and appreciate your unique place in the world. Next you need to tune into your essence and find joy, by letting go of the rules, the roles, and the "shoulds" that limit you.

In the *Increase Your Self-Knowledge* section of C: Compliment and Nurture you explored the roles that define you: parent, spouse, daughter, cousin, teacher, artist, and others. Using roles to define you is grounding because roles offer structure to your life. Roles communicate information about who you are, but roles also communicate information about who you aren't, so therefore, roles can also be self-limiting.

Evelyn was newly married. In her role as a single co-ed she went out to lunch with friends, attended concerts and stayed up late watching horror movies. *As a married woman, she felt compelled to adopt the role of "wife," which involved pinching pennies, staying in to watch TV, learning to cook, and cleaning incessantly. Evelyn had lost touch with her fun-loving essence. She had narrowed herself in her new role as wife. Is it any wonder that she started to move down the path to despair?*

Do you limit yourself in the roles you play? Are there parts of you that you hide for fear of stepping out of the box and letting the real you be visible? One way to tune into how you limit yourself is to pay attention to when you use "shoulds" and "woulds": A good parent "should."... A responsible husband "would"... Try filling in the blanks using your own roles. See how you disconnect from your essence by letting your roles limit you. When you lose contact with your essence, joy eludes you because it's hard to be happy and hopeful when you feel constricted and cut off.

Hope involves energy so connecting with your essence also requires action. Acting brings you into the present and takes you off the path to despair. It's hard to do something active with your body while your mind is somewhere else. Express yourself through writing, building, drawing, talking, exercising, creating, cooking, or doing anything that gets you moving. What activities bring you joy? Make time for them because engaging in activities involves energy, and connecting with your essence requires action.

Remember the adage, "all work and no play makes Jack a dull boy"? It's true. Individuals with many interpersonal connections handle adversity better, adapt to change more easily, and indulge in addictive behavior less often. Engaging in a variety of activities like clubs or sports, or developing friendships, provides a support system that you can rely on in times of stress. Activities offer healthy and functional distractions. Individuals who experience mood instability often feel like crawling into bed and pulling the covers over their heads, but movement can often be the best medicine. For example, Todd looked forward to an evening session of yoga after work to reduce stress, and Brenda wouldn't miss racquetball with the girls for the same reason. Both activities helped Todd and Brenda to feel good about their lives by directing their energy outward.

Actively turning inward also has benefits. Take some time just to be with yourself, like a status check. An evening walk around the neighborhood can be just enough to connect you with your unique essence. Meditating or journaling regularly are other great ways to stay in touch with what is happening inside you. Without censoring your thoughts, simply write in your journal whatever is on your mind. Anything that comes to mind about your life is worthy of being written down. Meditating is like journaling without the paper. Be still and comfortable in a place where you won't be disturbed and notice where your thoughts go and what comes into your mind. Simply notice your thoughts without attaching a judgment, without associating an intention; just simply notice what comes up from inside you when you are quiet and still enough to hear. Journaling and meditating are opportunities to be present in your life.

Another way to generate hope and connect with your essence is by making plans, big plans, which keeps your eye intentionally focused on the future. Although it is helpful to break down these big plans into manageable chunks that you can work on step by step, thinking big boosts hope. Don't be afraid to think big. Remember that the world holds an abundance of good things, there is enough to go around, and you are entitled to your share.

> Barry opened a small coffee shop and focused on the nuts and bolts of managing a single restaurant, but his partner, Randall, helped him see the big picture. Randall encouraged Barry to see that by developing their own restaurant theme and management style they could simplify their efforts to franchise in the future.

Finally, connecting with your essence takes forgiveness, not from someone else, but from you. Forgive yourself for not being perfect, for not always making the best of every opportunity offered to you, and for simply being human. We've talked before about putting away your personal plan of improvement and connecting with your essence, which involves loving yourself just as you are, just as you have been, and just as you will be. You are who you are and you really can't be anyone else, so why not enjoy being you? It's certainly easier that way. Fully enjoy your life, every minute of every day, as much as is possible. Don't give away any of the power that you have in being alive. Embrace your life and your unique essence wholeheartedly. Be fully present with your life, and there will be no room for despair to take a seat and get comfortable. When positive energy is guiding your life, despair recedes. You'll simply have no place for negative thoughts if you are involved in building your dreams. Life is meant to be enjoyed in small ways each and every day. Try something new today!

Charge Up Exercise Three
Hope and Dream

Find your positive energy by exploring the following:

1. Notice those activities, persons, foods, smells, sounds, and environments that give you pleasure and yield positive energy. What experiences at work, home, and other places bring you joy?

_____

_____

_____

_____

_____

2. On the flip side, notice those activities, persons, foods, smells, sounds, and environments that negate or diminish your energy. List those items below that create negative energy.

_____

_____

_____

_____

_____

_____

3. How can you reduce or eliminate some of the negatives that you identified above?

_____

_____

_____

_____

4. How can you increase access to the positives that you identified in #1? What positive energy can you incorporate into your life this week?

_____

_____

_____

_____

5. What "big plans" and dreams can you imagine in your life? Remember to think as "Big" as you can. What do you desire?

_____

_____

_____

_____

_____

_____

E – Enjoy and Experience Life

Step Four: Live in Harmony

Charles Darwin understood interconnectedness when he said that "cat-loving spinsters make London a beautiful place to live." He explained that the number of cats in London kept the number of mice under control. The mice, in turn, were not able to disturb the underground nests of bees, which were then able to pollinate more freely, resulting in more beautiful gardens in London. Each piece of this chain was necessary to achieve the end.

Every thought, feeling, and action has a ripple effect in the world. Nothing happens in isolation; all living beings are interconnected, as we're reminded by the famous John Donne quote, "No man is an island." The kind word that you say to the clerk at the mini-mart on the way to work is passed on by the clerk in good feelings and kind words toward another person. The unkind words spoken to a fellow driver with a raised fist can contribute to a bad day because you are affected by everyone around you. Interconnectedness, and specifically the quality of your connections, impacts you and, in turn, the universe.

Thich Nhat Han, a Buddhist monk, said that when a poet looks at his work, he sees a cloud. He meant that clouds bring rain, which allows more trees to grow, which then are used to make paper. The interconnectedness of the universe is apparent to the writer and poet.

These lovely examples show how living beings do not exist in isolation but are part of a chain that affects the individual as well as the universe as a whole. Along the same lines, the work of internationally renowned Japanese scientist Masaru Emoto revealed that molecules of water are affected by our thoughts, words, and feelings. Through his experiments, he discovered that ice crystals developed in different ways depending on their environment. When loving, positive thoughts were directed to them and kind words said near them, the crystals became clear and symmetrical. If, however, angry words were spoken and unkind thoughts directed at them, the crystals became dull and asymmetrical. He concluded that even at the molecular level, we are affected by our surroundings, and as we have already stated, every thought, feeling and word has an effect on us. It also affects the world around us.

When you recognize the interconnectedness of all humanity, you show respect for the living environment as a whole. You see that we are connected on a molecular level as humans, so what we do to others we do to ourselves. Human beings are hardwired for interconnectedness, and we intrinsically understand that there are personal consequences when we harm one another. Interconnectedness extends beyond the person-to-person level and reaches across countries because everything you do affects yourself and others in both positive and negative ways. What you do matters, everything from how you act toward individuals you meet, all the way to how factories run in foreign lands, has an impact on the environment around you.

More than ever, people today are interested in learning a second or third language, and worldwide travel has markedly increased. This desire to connect with others in faraway places decreases the distance between all of us. Hollywood personalities adopt children from Asia and Africa. Musicians group together for benefit concerts to reduce world hunger. Individuals who care about the welfare of people they have never met start nongovernmental and nonprofit organizations. Problems in one area of the world are often solved by international collaboration. You are connected by your humanity to every other person. You may recognize intellectually that you live in a global economy, but human interdependence is much more complex and multi-faceted than just "doing business." When individuals suffer in one part of the world, the ramifications of their distress travel throughout the rest of world and impact people in distant countries.

Humanity lives on planet earth, your only home. You have finite resources, and you are entrusted with using them responsibly. There are many ways to live green through your purchases of clothing, cars, and home products. Conservation, planting trees, global warming, renewable sources of energy, overpopulation, and depletion of natural resources are only a few of the issues facing humanity today. Caring about your environment and living green not only preserves your resources for future generations, but also shows a deep respect for the bountiful universe you are privileged to live in.

When you recognize your interconnection with the universe, you understand that the loss of your presence is a loss for every other living being. You are necessary. Your presence completes the whole and your absence diminishes the whole. Each person occupies a space in time that cannot be filled by another person. No one can be replaced because each person is unique and necessary in his or her own way. All living beings have self-worth; are connected to one another; deserve love, happiness, and success; and share a common desire for a joyful life. You will experience the true love, happiness, and success you deserve when you reach out in positive ways to others.

What can you do to preserve the bounty of the world? How can you reach out into the world in a humanitarian way? Demonstrate that you understand how interconnectedness works in the world and you will enrich your life in unexpected ways. Reaching beyond your personal experience into the world, in a meaningful and ethical way, builds hope in you and spreads its effect everywhere.

Charge Up Exercise Four
Live in Harmony!

Practice living in harmony by doing the following:

1. In what small ways can you to spread "kind words" and positive regard to others on a daily basis?

_____

_____

_____

_____

_____

2. What small actions can you take to create a better environment for your neighborhood, state, country, or planet? Make a list of what you are currently doing and think of other things that may be added.

_____

_____

_____

_____

_____

3. What groups can you start or join that can make an impact on others' lives? What part of your world would you like to impact most?

_____

_____

_____

_____

_____

_____

4. List three small ways that you can start to make a difference in the world today?

_____

_____

_____

_____

_____

_____

E: Enjoy and Experience Life

Now that you have finished E: Enjoy and Experience Life, what skills have you learned and what ones are you still working on?

* Put a check mark in front of the statements that feel true to you right now.
* Mark a circle in front of the statements that you have not yet achieved.

____ I deserve love, happiness, and success.

____ I recognize that feeling helpless, hopeless, and passive can lead to despair.

____ I believe that I am an important part of a greater whole.

____ I live life as an adventure that is meant to be enjoyed.

____ I seek out many interests, and I take time to enjoy them.

____ Connecting with others is energizing and fulfilling for me.

____ I avoid personalizing situations because I know that everything isn't about me.

____ I recognize when distractions become addictions and ways I avoid life.

____ I believe that we are all connected by our humanity.

____ I recognize that how my life is going is my responsibility.

_____ I make big plans that keep me focused on being positive and direct my energy out into the world.

_____ I avoid catastrophizing by keeping events in perspective.

_____ I connect to my positive energy when I avoid being confined by roles.

_____ I connect with the world through positive language and good will.

_____ I avoid filtering and black-and-white thinking by focusing on the positive and staying hopeful.

_____ I am practicing using "E: Enjoy and Experience Life," in the following ways.

_____

_____

_____

_____

_____

_____

_____

_____

_____

_____

_____

_____

E – Enjoy and Experience Life

Additional Resources

The following is a list of suggested materials to help you on your journey to enjoying your life and feeling hopeful:

* *Learned Optimism: How to Change Your Mind and Your Life* by Martin E. P. Seligman – easy-to-follow techniques to boost your mood, rise above pessimism, and change your internal negative dialogue.

* *The Art of Happiness: A Handbook for Living* by His Holiness the Fourteenth Dalai Lama – teaches how to feel connected to your fellow human beings and to your world by living a life of compassion.

* *The Element: How Finding Your Passion Changes Everything* by Ken Robinson – pursuing work that is aligned with your individual talents and passions is the route to success and well-being.

* *Being Happy: A Handbook to Greater Confidence and Security* by Andrew Matthews – An easy-to-read book which provides an understanding of things that gets in the way of living happily.

* *Permission to Dream Journal: Write, Collage, and Play Your Way to Living the Life of Your Dreams* by Lisa Hammond – Discover and create a positive and fulfilling life.

* *Happiness: Essential Mindful Practices* by Thich Nhat Han - through mindfulness you can learn to live in the present moment and develop a sense of peace for yourself and the world.

"I keep the telephone of my mind open to peace, harmony, health, love and abundance. Then whenever doubt, anxiety, or fear try to call me, they keep getting a busy signal and soon they'll forget my number."

—Edith Armstrong

Author

Summary and Final Words

The goal for all living beings is to find love, happiness, and success. We hope that becoming aware of the six barriers, working through the exercises, and applying the six solutions have helped you move forward on your journey to living the life you want and deserve.

We invite you to check out these other titles in our Charge Up Your Life self-help series:

* Charge Up Your Life Workbook, over 100 tools to explore and discover the real you
* Charge Up Your Life Journal, Guided Daily Writings
* Charge Up Your Life for Teens and Young Adults, due out spring 2011
* Charge Up Your Life for Parents, due out fall 2011

Glossary of Terms

1. **0-2 Response Check:** 167, 173, 176

   A rating of self-expression where an individual earns one point for expressing an opinion, two points for being validated, and zero points for remaining silent.

2. **AAA Method:** 138, 139

   A tool for conversation where an individual first *acknowledges* the speaker's point of view, next *asks* pertinent questions, before finally offering any *advice*.

3. **Addictive Behavior:** 192, 205, 206, 210

   Chronic and repetitive behaviors which temporarily distract you from people or situations which you find troubling.

4. **Adopt Social Perspective:** 143

   Considering another's person's point of view on any given subject.

5. **Anchors:** 80, 81, 91, 93-95, 101-103, 106, 107

   The traits with which you most closely identify.

6. **Anxiety: 25, 26, 43, 44, 46-48, 50-56, 58, 60-61**

Fear of the unknown, which takes you unintentionally out of the present into the past or the future.

7. **Apprehension: 44, 50, 58**

Fears over the future.

8. **Bank Account of Virtues: 22, 30**

A listing of positive attributes and items about yourself.

9. **Behavioral Excesses: 26**

Engaging in dysfunctional behaviors to an extreme, such as drugs, alcohol, eating, gambling, spending, sex, work, and exercise in an attempt to bolster low self-esteem.

10. **Black and White Thinking: 143**

Viewing the world in terms of clear definitions of right and wrong with little or no regard for extenuating circumstances. Lacks any middle ground view of other possibilities.

11. **Body Check: 177**

Saying out loud what you are thinking, feeling, or planning to do, to see if it feels true in your gut.

12. **Body Scan: 57**

Noticing each part of your body, from head to toe, to check for negative feelings and tension.

13. Body Talk: 44, 52-59, 61, 68, 85, 104, 177, 178

Stress related bodily complaints which can range from vague aches and pains to serious medical conditions.

14. Catastrophize: 196, 200

Magnifying the importance and intensity of an event beyond what is reasonable.

15. Catastrophe Rating: 59

Using a 1 to 10 rating scale to assess the importance of worrisome events, with a 10 representing the most catastrophic thing that you could ever imagine happening, and a one representing something for which you have minimal concern.

16. Circle of Integrity: 61, 157, 161, 164, 165, 167, 179

An imaginary circle that contains your positive traits, skills, attributes, values, and beliefs.

17. Common Human Traits: 121, 125, 126

Personality characteristics which are shared by all humans, such as seeking happiness and avoiding pain.

18. Compassion: 119, 122, 143

Understanding someone else's feelings and perspective.

19. Compromise: 49, 118

Arriving at a solution on which both parties can agree.

20. Cumulative Worry Rating: 60

A rating from 1-10 representing the amount of worry, frustration, and fear that you can comfortably handle on a regular basis.

21. Depressive Thinking: 194, 208

Viewing the world in a negative or limiting way by catastrophizing, personalizing, or filtering.

22. Dream Guide: Houses: 86, 87

Exploring how houses are depicted in your dreams to determine how you are feeling about yourself at the time of the dream.

23. Dream Guide: Water: 55

Exploring how large and small bodies of water are depicted in your dreams to determine the intensity of emotions in your life at the time of the dream.

24. Dream Guide: Transportation: 204, 205

Exploring how modes of transportation are depicted in your dreams to determine your level of motivation at the time of the dream.

25. Emotional Contact: 134, 137–139

Understanding the feelings and emotional perspective of the speaker.

26. Emotional Residue: 176

Feelings of regret or discomfort which persist after a decision has been made.

27. Empathy: 122

Showing compassion by understanding the point of view of another, seeing their common human qualities.

28. Fear of Failure: 192, 201

Worry over not succeeding which interferes with attaining goals.

29. Fear of Success: 192, 202, 203

Worry over how your life may change if you reach your goal.

30. Filtering: 197,200

Overfocusing on the negative elements of a situation and minimizing the positive elements.

31. Gestalt Therapy Theory: xv, 185

A type of therapy that focuses upon the individual's experience in the present moment and the self-regulating adjustments people make to adapt. It is a holistic approach to mind, body, and culture.

32. Golden Rule: 121, 122

Do unto others as you would have them do unto you.

33. Grief: 50, 53, 54, 58, 72

Sorrow after a loss.

34. Guilt: 80, 96–99, 143, 171

A feeling that you have done something wrong.

35. Interconnected Living: 178, 179, 215–217

Being connected to and interdependent with various life systems and organisms.

36. Intentional Distractions: 205, 206, 208

Productive and necessary breaks from lengthy or challenging tasks.

37. Interpersonal Boundary: 156

The point where your identity stops and makes contact with the identity of another person.

38. I-Statements / You-Statements: 135, 136

Owning your words by use of the word "I."

Deflecting ownership of words by using the collective "You" or accusing someone in an aggressive manner.

39. I-Thou vs I-It Relationship (Martin Buber): 123, 124, 126, 135

Contends that human life finds its meaningfulness in relationships. I-It relationships are vertical in nature where the "other" is objectified and dehumanized. I-Thou relationships are horizontal in nature and are positive, respectful, and human-to-human.

40. Mental Contact: 135, 136

Involves communicating effectively on a cognitive level by choosing your words, taking ownership of your thoughts and opinions, checking out assumptions, and asking clarifying questions.

41. Mind Reading: 141–143

Assuming that you know what someone is thinking without checking it out with them.

42. Narcissist: 173

Extremely self-interested people who cannot see the perspective of anyone but themselves.

43. Paradoxical Theory of Change: xv, 111

The paradox is that the more one attempts to be who one is not, the more one remains the same. Put another way, change comes about as a result of "fully accepting and embracing who you are," rather than by striving to be different.

44. Personal Filter: 18, 86, 127, 128, 136, 195, 198

Your unique and individual way of viewing the world which is represented in your thoughts, feelings, and behavior.

45. Personalizing: 196, 198, 200

Believing that an event or a remark is about you when it is not.

46. Physical Contact: 34, 134, 135

Using your body to communicate by smiling, nodding, and making eye contact.

47. Planning: 48, 167

Intentionally looking into the future in preparation.

48. Procrastination: 98, 192, 203, 204

When you delay acting to avoid a challenging event.

49. Reciprocity: 141, 144

The expectation of repayment for a kindness.

50. Resentment: 176

Feelings of bitterness or anger following a response which you regret.

51. Resistance: 104

Internal conflict when you try to make changes which are contrary to your essence.

52. Reviewing: 48

Intentionally looking back over events to assess or reminisce.

53. Rumination: 44, 50

Unintentionally being pulled into the past to relive troubling events.

54. Sand and Ocean Metaphor: 129, 156

Metaphor for establishing interpersonal contact using the point where the ocean and the sand meet; they blend but retain their unique essence.

55. Self-Esteem: xv, 9-11, 15, 16, 18, 25-27, 29, 30, 37, 173

A person's overall evaluation or appraisal of his or her own worth, not confined to simply recognizing strengths but, instead, embracing and appreciating the whole person.

56. Sensory Check-in: 66–68

Evaluation of each sense (sight, sound, taste, touch, and smell) in order to establish contact with your body in the present.

57. Shame: 14–16, 24, 29, 30, 43, 80, 81, 96–100, 102–104, 110, 143, 164–167, 170

Feeling that you are wrong at your essence.

58. Shoulds and Woulds: 100, 209, 210

Shaming words which communicate that you are not doing something correctly.

59. Simple Self-Expression: 166

The primary goal of self-support, to express who you are at your essence in an authentic manner.

60. Sociopath: 173, 185

Pathologically self-interested individuals who understand right and wrong, but exploit others in order to meet their own needs.

61. Temperament: 84, 85, 91, 93, 105, 110, 118, 127–129, 156

Traits of behavior which are innate, such as adaptability to change, level of physical activity, frustration tolerance, intensity of reactions, quality of mood, persistence, sociability, and distractibility.

62. Traits: 10, 13, 17, 21, 79–82, 84–91, 93–97, 99, 100, 102–104, 106, 107, 119–121, 125–127, 133, 158, 159, 162, 163, 179

Habitual patterns of behavior, thought, and emotion.

63. Triggers: 30, 80, 81, 96–104, 106, 107, 143, 170, 171

The traits that cause you to feel shame and guilt.

64. Worry Rating: 59

Assessment of your concerns on a scale from 1-10.

65. You-Statements: 142

Accusations involving mind-reading which elicit defensiveness in the other person.

C.H.A.R.G.E. Up Your Life

Reading Group Guide

It takes a lot of courage to show your dreams
to someone else.

-Erma Bombeck

Reading Group Guide

Charge Up Your Life Groups are designed to help individuals work together to increase self-awareness, self-confidence, and personal growth. The materials are based on the Charge Up Your Life model which offers tools to help individuals manage life's challenges and conquer the barriers that hold them back. Together, group members reinforce one another as they discover new insights to reach their personal goals.

Materials:

* Book: *Charge Up Your Life: Conquer the 6 Barriers to Love, Happiness and Success.*

* Workbook: (optional) *Charge Up Your Life Workbook: over 100 tools to explore and discover the real you.*

* Journal: (optional) *Charge Up Your Life Journal: Guided Daily Writings,* in which to keep notes, ideas, and exercises.

Setting Up the Group:

* Gather a group of 3-6 individuals who are interested in self-exploration and personal growth.

* Select people who are willing to meet on a regular basis and who can commit to the following group guidelines:
   o Respect the privacy and confidentiality of other group members.
   o Give positive feedback and support to self and others.
   o Refrain from giving advice.
   o Be open to numerous possibilities.
   o Encourage members to share their successes and strug-

gles, even though the intent of the group is not therapy of any kind.

- o Decide on a schedule that works for everyone. Some groups may decide on 1-2 times per week while another group may find that every other week works best.
- o Allow enough time between sessions to practice and integrate the concepts.

Book Layout:

The book is designed with 6 chapters corresponding to each of the 6 key solutions in the acronym CHARGE. In addition, within each chapter there are four steps, so there are 24 steps in all. Each step has its own exercise and each chapter has an exercise to introduce the main concept. Below is a condensed and easy-to-follow outline of the CHARGE Up Your Life model:

	The Phrase and Focus	The Barrier	The Solution
C	Compliment and Nurture	Self-Criticism	Self-Nurturance
H	Here and Now	Anxiety and Stress	Focused Awareness
A	Accept Your Possibilities	Self-Limiting Beliefs	Unlimited Possibilities
R	Respectful Relationships	Conflict	Harmony
G	Genuine and Authentic	Unhealthy Boundaries	Integrity
E	Enjoy and Experience Life	Despair	Hope

Group Sessions:

The number of sessions will depend on the needs of your group and the depth in which you want to cover each topic. In order for the best use of this material in the fewest number of sessions, we recommend a total of **14 Sessions:** one-half chapter per session (12), one session for the introduction and quiz, and a final session for closure, self-discovery, and future intentions. Of course, feel free to divide the material in the way that works best for you. The suggested sessions that follow can be easily modified to fit your schedule.

Companion Workbook:

The CHARGE Up Your Life Companion Workbook provides additional exercises for each section in the book. If more practice on a particular issue is needed, the workbook may be used within the group for deeper understanding and discussion, independently between sessions, or as a follow-up book when the main book is completed.

Session Guide

Session One: Introduction and Quiz:

Preparation:

1. Read the Book's Introduction.

2. Take the Charge Up Your Life Quiz. Score it and bring your results to the first meeting.

3. Purchase or create a journal to use throughout the book.

Group Discussion Points:

* Identify the strengths and challenges revealed in the quiz.
* Were the results surprising? Why or why not?
* In what area of your life do the challenges you identified hold you back: home life, work, friends, with extended family?
* Which of these items in the quiz would you like to focus on?

* What area is the most interesting to you? Why?

Session Two: Chapter C: Compliment and Nurture (Part 1)

Preparation:

1. Read the introduction to C.

2. Read and do The Nurturing Parent Experience. Write about your insights and experiences in your journal.

3. Read Step One: Know Your Worth and Step Two: Increase Your Self-Knowledge. Do the exercises that follow each one.

Group Discussion Points:

* As you read the stories about Sam and Myra, in what ways could you relate to them? What personal barriers could you identify within each story?
* Do you feel unique and irreplaceable? Why or why not?
* What did you discover about yourself in the Nurturing Parent Experience?
* What guide did you choose? Explain and discuss.
* How do you define your worth? Is it contingent on a product?
* In what ways do you relate to Christoper Reeve, Kathy, Cindy Crawford, or Elle Woods?
* How do you contribute to the world in your own unique way? How is the world changed because of you?
* In what ways do you relate to Vicki, Debbie, June, Chun, Greg, or Yesenia?
* How easy was it for you to start your Bank Account of Virtues journal? How well do you know yourself? Do you need to take more time to learn your preferences, thoughts, needs, and desires?

Session Three: Chapter C: Compliment and Nurture (Part 2)

Preparation:

1. Read Step Three: Strengthen Your Self-Support and Step Four: Appreciate Yourself. Do the exercises that follow each one.

2. Fill out the Self-Check Milestones and bring results to group.

3. Look over the Resource Page. Which ones would you like to pursue?

Group Discussion Points:

* In what ways do you support yourself physically, mentally, emotionally, and spiritually?

* What was your experience in doing the activities on strengthening self-support?

* In what ways do you show appreciation for yourself and allow yourself to receive the good things in life?

* In what ways could you relate to Jade, Johnna, or Beth in regard to receiving praise, money, acceptance, fame, and so on?

* What was your experience in doing the activities on self-appreciation?

* What milestones have you accomplished and which ones need more practice?

* Did any quotations in this chapter have meaning for you or inspire you in some way?

* What resources could you add to the list in the book that would strengthen self-love, confidence, and esteem?

Session Four: Chapter H: Here and Now (Part 1)

Preparation:

1. Read the introduction to H.

2. Read and do Safe and Tranquil Experience. Write about your insights and experiences in your journal.

3. Read Step One: Know Where You Are and Step Two: Listen to Your Body Talk. Do the exercises that follow each one.

Group Discussion Points:

*   In what ways do anxiety and stress affect your life?
*   Share your Safe and Tranquil place with the group. What did you discover about yourself by doing this exercise?
*   How much time do you spend in the present in any given day? Are your worries past or future oriented?
*   In what ways do you relate to Marilyn, Connie, Haley, Kirsten, or Amos?
*   How does your body talk to you? How good are you at paying attention to your body talk?
*   In what ways do you relate to Regina, Brian, or Michele?
*   How effective are you at relieving your stress once you notice body talk?

Session Five: Chapter H: Here and Now (Part 2)

Preparation:

1. Read Step Three: Keep Situations Right-Sized and Step Four: Stay Grounded through Your Senses. Do the exercises that follow each one.

2. Do the Self-Check Milestones and bring results to group.

3. Look over the Resource Page. Which ones would you like to pursue?

Group Discussion Points:

* In what ways have you experienced or noticed someone else displaying big feelings that were incongruent with the actual situation?

* Discuss your dream experiences that contain water.

* Can you relate to Betty's situation? Share a time you experienced something similar.

* In what ways can the 0-2 response check technique help to reduce anxiety?

* What did you discover about yourself in doing the activities on keeping things right-sized?

* In what ways can you practice staying grounded and present in your life?

* Kelly and Morgan have found ways to manage anxiety and stay focused. Share some techniques that you use.

* What was your experience in doing the activities on staying grounded through your senses?

* What milestones have you accomplished and which ones need more practice?

* Did any quotations in this chapter have meaning for you or inspire you in some way?

* What resources could you add to the list in the book that would reduce stress and anxiety and help you stay focused in the present?

Session Six: Chapter A: Accept Your Possibilities (Part 1)

Preparation:

1. Read the introduction to A.

2. Read and do Famous Person Experience. Write about your insights and experiences in your journal.

3. Read Step One: Notice Every Trait and Step Two: Be Proud of Your Anchors. Do the exercises that follow each one.

Group Discussion Points:

- In what ways do you define yourself and in what ways do you limit yourself?
- What did you learn about yourself in doing the Famous Person Experience? What are the traits you notice in others?
- What traits from the trait box do you recognize in yourself?
- In what ways do you relate to Loretta, Kitty, Ethan, Emma, or Sheila?
- Discuss your dream experiences which include houses in them.
- What were your experiences in doing the activities on noticing every trait?
- What are your anchors? How do you feel about each one of them?
- In what ways do you relate to Brooke, Luke, Ian, or Aaron?
- Who are the people throughout your life who have been most influential in developing your anchors?

Session Seven: Chapter A: Accept Your Possibilities (Part 2)

Preparation:

1. Read Step Three: Understand Your Triggers and read Step Four: Use All Your Traits. Do the exercises that follow each one.

2. Do the Self-Check Milestones and bring results to group.

3. Look over the Resource Page. Which ones would you like to pursue?

Group Discussion Points:

* Talk about your experiences being triggered or shamed. How do these experiences affect your daily life?

* In what ways can you relate to the triggers and shame experienced by Joyce, Dana, Dorrie, or Chad?

* How do you feel when someone uses the following words: "should," "have to," "always," and "never" or judgment words such as "good," "bad, "right," or "wrong"?

* What traits in the Trait Box could you make more use of? Which traits do you overuse?

* In what ways did you relate to Coreen's, Richard's, and Suzanne's stories?

* Talk about your experiences doing the activities on using all your traits.

* What milestones have you accomplished and which ones need more practice?

* Did any quotations in this chapter have meaning for you or inspire you in some way?

* What resources could you add to the list in the book that would help you increase the possibilities in your life?

Session Eight: Chapter R: Respectful Relationships (Part 1)

Preparation:

1. Read the introduction to R.

2. Read and do The **Ambassador** Experience. Write about your insights and experiences in your journal.

3. Read Step One: Recognize Similarities and Step Two: Acknowledge Differences. Do the exercises that follow each one.

Group Discussion Points:

- Which relationships are going well for you and which ones would you like to improve?

- What was the Ambassador Experience like for you? What traits would you need to develop? What did you discover about yourself?

- In your circle of family and friends, what similarities do you see?

- How can you relate to the stories of Frank, Satinder, Eugene, and Elizabeth?

- Talk about your experiences doing the activities on recognizing similarities in others.

- Do you find that your personal filter interferes with your ability to relate to others? Talk about when you've noticed this.

- Talk about how you relate to the stories of Stan, Maria, or Patrick.

- Talk about your experiences doing the activities on acknowledging differences.

Session Nine: Chapter R: Respectful Relationships (Part 2)

Preparation:

1. Read Step Three: Interact with Diplomacy and Step Four: Establish Trust. Do the exercises that follow each one.

2. Do the Self-Check Milestones and bring results to group.

3. Look over the Resource Page. Which ones would you like to pursue?

Group Discussion Points:

- In what ways do you use diplomacy in your life? In what situations would you like your use of diplomacy to improve?

- Talk about how you relate to the stories of Celia, Matthew, Tara, Austin, or Terry.

- Talk about a time when you could have used the AAA Method.

- Talk about your experiences doing the activities on interacting with diplomacy.

- In which relationships have you established trust and in which relationships do you wish to build trust?

- How can you relate to the stories of Bernadette, Charlene, Lucinda, David, Carson, Arthur, or Adam?

- What insight did you acquire in doing the activities on establishing trust?

- What milestones have you accomplished and which ones need more practice?

- Did any quotations in this chapter have meaning for you or inspire you in some way?

- What resources could you add to the list in the book that would help you create trustful interpersonal relationships?

Session Ten: Chapter G: Genuine and Authentic (Part 1)

Preparation:

1. Read the introduction to G.

2. Read and do **Being in Your Circle Experience**. Write about your insights and experiences in your journal.

3. Read Step One: Know What You Stand For and Step Two: Acknowledge Differences. Do the exercises that follow each one.

Group Discussion Points:

- How authentic do you feel your relationships are with the people you are closest to?

- What was the Being in Your Circle Experience like for you? What traits would you like to develop? What did you discover about yourself?

- In what relationships do you feel you have a strong sense of self with healthy boundaries? In what interpersonal relationships would you like to strengthen this ability?

- Which of the stories did you identify with most closely: Becky, Susan B. Anthony, Paula, Clint Eastwood, or Jackie?

- Share your personal identity statement. How good are you at expressing each part of it in your life? Where could you improve?

- How good are you at expressing and supporting your personal preferences? With whom do you experience the greatest difficulty?

- In what ways do you relate to Taylor, Gemma, or Betsy?

- In what setting do you live with the most integrity: home, work, or with friends?

Session Eleven: Chapter G: Genuine and Authentic (Part 2)

Preparation:

1. Read Step Three: Handle External Pressure and Step Four: Make Ethical Choices. Do the exercises that follow each one.

2. Do the Self-Check Milestones and bring results to group.

3. Look over the Resource Page. Which ones would you like to pursue?

Group Discussion Points:

- In what ways are you pulled out of your circle?
- Share how you related to one of the stories in this section: Hillary, Joyce, Anthony, Ron, or Mercedes.
- From what areas or from what people do you experience the most external pressures in your life? How do you handle it?

- How can you relate to the dilemmas experienced by Jack, Tim, Angie, or Eaton?

- Discuss some other ethical choices that you encounter on a daily basis?

- What milestones have you accomplished and which ones need more practice?

- Did any quotations in this chapter have meaning for you or inspire you in some way?

- What resources could you add to the list in the book that would help you increase authentic visibility with yourself and others?

Session Twelve: Chapter E: Enjoy and Experience Life (Part 1)

Preparation:

1. Read the introduction to E.

2. Read and do the World Market Experience. Write about your insights and experiences in your journal.

3. Read Step One: Notice Negativity and Step Two: Let Yourself Be Happy. Do the exercises that follow each one.

Group Discussion Points:

- In what ways do you stop yourself from truly enjoying life?

- Talk about the gift you received in the World Market Experience and its meaning for you.

- When have you experienced depressive thinking or despair?

- Share how you related to one of the stories in this section: Harry, Marlon, Mia, Tasha,Corbin, Eddie, Olivia, or Maxine.

- Which type of negative thinking is the most difficult for you to overcome: filtering, catastrophizing, or personalizing? Talk about your experiences.

- Do you believe there is enough happiness to go around in the world? What do you need in your life to be happy?
- With which of the following stories can you most closely identify: Natalie, Russell, Jim, Tammy, Emily, Wayne, Paul, or Victoria. How do you set yourself up for failure?
- Discuss your dream experiences that include modes of transportation.
- How good are you at allowing yourself to be happy? Do you believe there's a balance sheet of unhappiness and happiness for each person?

Session Thirteen: Chapter E: Enjoy and Experience Life (Part 2)

Preparation:

1. Read Step Three: Hope and Dream and Step Four: Live in Harmony. Do the exercises that follow each one.

2. Do the Self-Check Milestones and bring results to group.

3. Look over the Resource Page. Which ones would you like to pursue?

Group Discussion Points:

- In what ways do you hold yourself back from pursuing your dreams?
- Choose one of the following stories and share how you identify with the character: Hannah, Evelyn, Todd, Brenda, Barry, or Randall.
- Share two of your BIG dreams.
- In what ways do you interconnect with and contribute to humanity and our planet?
- How harmonious is your environment? What do you do personally to make a contribution to harmony at home and at work?

- What milestones have you accomplished and which ones need more practice?
- Did any quotations in this chapter have meaning for you or inspire you in some way?
- What resources could you add to the list in the book that would help you increase your happiness and positive impact in the world?

Session Fourteen: Closure, Self-Discovery, Intentions

Preparation:

1. Read through your journal.

2. Review your milestones from each of the six chapters.

3. Reread any sections you missed or need to review.

Group Discussion Points:

- In what ways was this book helpful to you on your journey to self-discovery?
- What areas from the book were especially helpful?
- What did you discover about yourself?
- In what ways have you changed?
- As you move forward, what intentions can you make to continue your growth? As you look back on your milestones, in what areas would you like more practice?
- What's one thing the group can do to support each member to continue on the path to love, happiness, and success?

Ellen is a psychologist with thirty years' experience working with adults, children, and families in public and private schools, first as a secondary English teacher and later as school psychologist. In addition, she is a Gestalt-trained individual, family, couples, and children's play therapist with 20 years as a private practitioner. El-len has published a number of articles on educational topics in scholarly journals, and has made presentations at national conferences in psychology and education, as well as been a guest on local radio. She is a member of the American Psychological Association, the Arizona Psychological Association, and American Mensa. Ellen was an adjunct faculty member in the graduate colleges of educational psychology at both Arizona State University and Northern Arizona University, and has also been an instructor in the Maricopa County Community College system. Ellen is a nationally certified school psychologist and for over 20 years she has served as a fieldwork and internship supervisor for school psychology students in local and national university programs. Prior to its closure in 2005, Ellen was on the faculty of the Gestalt Institute of Phoenix.

Ellen raised three successful children as a single parent and so has special interests in mentoring other women in transition and helping parents to raise resilient children. Her background in education fostered an additional interest in helping teachers create emotionally safe classrooms to facilitate optimal learning. Ellen lives with her husband in the Phoenix area, where she enjoys hiking in the many nature preserves, spending time with her grandchildren, and volunteering in community outreach organizations for women and children.

Ellen can be contacted through her website www.ellendiana.com or through email at ellenmdiana@yahoo.com to provide feedback on books in the Charge Up Your Life series, or for information on psychological services and workshops focused on exploring women's issues or acquiring effective parenting skills.

Connie Leach is an author, speaker, and certified life coach who specializes in helping people realize their greatest potential in order to live their best lives. She strongly believes that everyone has their own unique gifts and capacity for success. Connie holds a bachelor's degree in psychology, master's degrees in elementary edu-cation and community counseling, and a doctorate degree in educational leadership along with extensive training in Gestalt therapy.

She spent much of her career as a teacher and administrator working with students living in high poverty and high crime areas in Phoenix. In addition, Connie served for several years as Arizona state president for the American Association of University Women, which fosters equity for women and girls. Connie continues working throughout the community, providing tools to assist women and teens in gaining insight, awareness, and self-discovery for lasting happiness and success. She has two adult children and currently resides in Scottsdale, Arizona, with her husband. Connie can be contacted through her website at www.connieleach.com or through email at conniemleach@yahoo.com.

CPSIA information can be obtained at www.ICGtesting.com
Printed in the USA
LVOW06s0127151113

361408LV00009B/270/P